FIRST FORM

STUDENT TEXT

Cheryl Lowe

First Form Latin
Student Text
by Cheryl Lowe

Published by:
Memoria Press
www.memoriapress.com

Cover: Coriolanus and the Women of Rome.

Discípulis et Paréntibus
(To the Students and Parents)

Congratulations! You are about to embark on a fascinating study of an amazing language. The Latin language is a model of order, clarity, and precision. With its declensions and conjugations marching in disciplined rows like Roman legions, there is no experience quite like learning the Latin grammar.

There are so many benefits to learning Latin, it is difficult to know where to start. I truly believe that Latin has more educational value than any other subject you can study. Here are a few things you will learn from Latin – the roots of English words, the roots of Western Civilization, how to think critically and logically, how to analyze, contrast, and compare, how to understand language, grammar, and words with a depth unknown to those who have never had the privilege of studying Latin. For the beginner, the greatest value of Latin is the mental training it provides, mental training that will carry over into all of your other subjects. With Latin you will learn how to learn, and you will become a better student in all of your other subjects.

And forget the old canard, *Latin is a dead language*. Latin is not dead, it's immortal! It is the most fruitful language in human history. It is the mother of the five Romance languages, French, Spanish, Portuguese, Italian, and Romanian. More than half of English words come from Latin. It is the language of the classification system for plants and animals. All of the modern sciences, from psychology to physics, derive most of their specialized vocabularies from Latin. It is the language of law and theology. When you learn Latin words you will be preparing yourself for almost any field of study you can imagine. Even the word *computer* comes from the Latin word for *I think, compute*, **computo**.

But the value of Latin is much more than the mental workout and vocabulary it provides. Latin is a journey. It can take you to the very height of what it means to be an educated person. You should get as much Latin as you can and whatever the amount, it will be of help to you. If you only take one year of Latin, you will benefit greatly. But I encourage you to study Latin as long as you can, until you have conquered it, and until you can read those classical authors whose books are still in print today, Caesar, Cicero, Ovid, and Vergil. I encourage you to persevere in your study of Latin until you have reached that summit of learning that *is* and *always* has been the *ideal* of the well-educated person.

It is a privilege to study Latin, and I encourage you to work hard and make the most of *this* opportunity, and *every* opportunity that comes to you in life.

Dominus vobiscum.
Cheryl Lowe

CONTENTS

The Dauntless Three
from
Horatius at the Bridge

Pronunciation

Latin pronunciation is very phonetic and regular. There are two major pronunciation systems, Christian (ecclesiastical) and Classical. This text uses Christian pronunciation because it is closer to modern English, is used in classical music and Christian prayers, and sounds more beautiful to the modern ear. In practice, there are only a few differences between the two, the most notable being that *v* is pronounced *v* in Christian Latin, and *w* in Classical. So, *veni, vidi, vici* becomes *weni, widi, wiki* in Classical Latin.

Fortunately, written Latin is the same regardless of the pronunciation. The following guide is for Christian pronunciation, but a Classical pronunciation guide is in the appendix.

Alphabet

The Latin alphabet has the same letters as English except that it has no **w**. The letters **y**, **z** and **k** are infrequent and usually found in words of Greek origin. The Roman letter **i** was both a vowel and a consonant (similar to the English **y**). The letter **j** was added during the Middle Ages for consonantal **i**. Thus **Iulius** and **Iesus** came to be written **Julius** and **Jesus**.

Vowels

Latin has long and short vowels, but the distinction between them is not always observed by English speakers. In this text we will focus on learning the long vowels and the consonants only. You will notice on the audio some vowels that tend toward the short sounds, so the short vowel sounds are given below. In this text, long vowels will not be marked with a macron except for a few inflected endings. [1]

long	as in	sound	example	short	as in	sound	example
ā	*fa*ther	/ah/	frāter	a	*a*gain	/uh/	mensa
ē	*la*te	/ā/ or /ay/	sēdēs	e	*E*d	/ĕ/	et
ī	*see*n	/ē/ or /ee/	amīcus	i	*i*t	/ĭ/	cibus
ō	*o*pen	/ō/ or /oh/	nōmen	o	*o*n	/ŏ/	novem
ū	*foo*d	/o͞o/	lūna	u	*foo*t	/o͝o/	sum

A helpful tip to remember the five long vowels is to learn the two words, **gloria** and **Jesu**.

The general rule for consecutive and double vowels is to give each vowel its proper sound with the following exceptions:

Digraphs

	as in	sound	example
ae and **oe**	*la*te	/ā/	caelum, proélium

Diphthong

	as in	sound	example
au	*ou*t	/ou/	laudo

6

Consonants

The Latin consonants have the same sounds as in English except as noted below. The rules for hard and soft **c** and **g** are usually true in English and always true in Latin. Note that soft **c** and **sc** have different sounds in English and Latin.

c, g, and **sc** are hard before **a, o, u,** and **consonants**

hard c as in **c**at	/k/	culpa, clamo
hard g as in **g**o	/g/	fuga, gloria
hard sc as in **sc**out	/sk/	scutum

c, g, and **sc** are soft before **e, i, ae, oe**

soft c as in **ch**arity	/ch/	caelum
soft g as in **g**em	/j/	regina
soft sc as in **sh**out	/sh/	scio

gn as in canyon	/ny/	pugno
ch is hard as in chemistry	/k/	choro
j as in **y**es	/y/	Jesus
s as in **s**ing, never as in nose /z/	/s/	mensa
t when followed by **i** and another vowel	/tsee/	gratia

Accents

For the beginning Latin student, the most helpful information is not long and short vowels, but rather knowing what syllable to accent. In this text you will always know the accented syllable by following these easy rules. The last three syllables in a Latin word have names.

a mi cus

antepenult (2nd last)   penult (next last)   ultima (last)

Ultima comes from *ultimus,* meaning the last, or ultimate. **Penult** comes from *penultima,* meaning next to last. **Antepenult** comes from *antepenultima,* meaning before the penult.

Latin words are always accented on either the penult or the antepenult, never on the last syllable. In this text, if the accent is on the penult it will not have an accent mark, but if the accent is on the antepenult it will have an accent mark.

am̲icus   but   **ámbulo**

accent on the penult - no mark   *accent on the antepenult - accent mark*

UNIT I INTRODUCTION

♦ In this unit you will learn *The Present System* of the *1st Conjugation* and the irregular verb **sum**.

♦ Latin verbs fall naturally into four groups or families called *conjugations*.

♦ Look at the conjugation of the present tense of the English verb *love*. Notice that the English verb *love* changes in the 3rd person singular which requires the ending **s**.

	SINGULAR	PLURAL
1st person *(person speaking)*	I love	we love
2nd person *(person spoken to)*	you love	you love
3rd person *(person spoken about)*	he, she, it <u>loves</u>	they love

♦ To *conjugate* a Latin verb is to say or write its forms in an organized chart similar to the one above.

♦ The six attributes of a Latin verb are: *conjugation, person, number, tense, voice,* and *mood*. In Latin, there are:

Four conjugations	1st, 2nd, 3rd, 4th
Three persons	first, second, and third persons
Two numbers	singular, plural
Six tenses	present, imperfect, future (Present System)
	perfect, pluperfect, future perfect (Perfect System)
Two voices	active and passive
Three moods	indicative, imperative, subjunctive

♦ In this unit you will learn about conjugation, person, number, and tense, but not voice and mood. (All verbs in this text are in the same voice and mood, *active indicative*.)

♦ Latin is a language of *stems* and *endings*. The three tenses of the Present System are all built on the *present stem*. The stem is the part of the word that doesn't change. The endings change for person, number, tense, voice, and mood.

UNIT I
VERBS
1ST CONJUGATION AND SUM

PRESENT SYSTEM

Romulus, Remus, and the She-wolf
Capitoline Museums, Rome

This iconic statue of the ancient city of Rome depicts the twin brothers, Romulus and Remus, suckled by a she-wolf. The myth that the Romans were descended from ancestors so fierce and courageous they were raised by a she-wolf fits the national character of Rome, a city chosen by destiny to conquer and rule the world. Romulus founded Rome and became her first king, giving Rome its name.

In choro recitemus. *Let us recite together.*

First Conjugation - Present Tense

present stem **ama-**

Person	Singular		Plural	
1st	am-**o**	I love	ama-**mus**	**we** love
2nd	ama-**s**	**you** (sing.) love	ama-**tis**	**you** (pl.) love
3rd	ama-**t**	**he, she, it** loves	ama-**nt**	**they** love

◆ **Amo** is our model to study *1st Conjugation* verbs.

◆ In the conjugation chart above the Latin *personal endings, o, s, t, mus, tis, nt,* are in bolded blue. The Latin personal endings correspond to the English personal pronouns.

◆ The *present tense* is formed by adding the personal endings to the *present stem,* **ama**.

◆ To find the *present stem* of each vocabulary word, drop the **o** and add **a,** the *stem vowel* of the first conjugation.[2]

Vocabulary

Latin	English	Derivatives
amo	I love, like	*amorous, amateur*
do	I give	*donate*
lavo	I wash	*lavatory*
nato	I swim	*natatorium*
oro	I speak, pray	*orator*
paro	I prepare	*preparation*
porto	I carry	*portable*
servo	I guard, keep	*conservation*
sto	I stand	*status*
voco	I call	*vocation, vocal*

◆ There are three persons in grammar. Below are the English pronouns and the corresponding Latin personal endings. Notice that English has only one word for the singular and plural **you**.

	SINGULAR		PLURAL	
First Person (person speaking)	I	o/m	we	mus
Second Person (person spoken to)	you (sing.)	s	you (pl.)	tis
Third Person (person spoken about)	he, she, it	t	they	nt

◆ The Latin present tense corresponds to the English *simple present, progressive present,* and *emphatic present.* In English **amo** can mean:

I love — simple present
I am loving — progressive present
I do love — emphatic present

Oral Drill

1. **amant** *they love*
2. **portat** *he carries*
3. **servo** *I gaurd*
4. **natamus** *we swim*
5. **lavas** *you wash*
6. **oratis** *Yall pray*
7. **dat** *he gives*
8. **stant** *they stand*
9. **paramus** *we prepare*
10. **vocas** *you call*

1. he is swimming *natat*
2. they pray *orant*
3. she washes *lavat*
4. you are guarding *servas*
5. he does give *dat*
6. we carry *portamus*
7. you (p) like *amatis*
8. we are calling *vocamus*
9. you stand *stas*
10. they prepare *parant*

Present

Simple — I love — amo
Emphatic — I do Love — amo
Progressive — I am Loving — amo

Context and Style

Stabat Mater   *The Mother was Standing*

First Conjugation - Imperfect Tense
present stem **ama-**

Singular		Plural	
ama-**bam**	I was loving	ama-**bamus**	we were loving
ama-**bas**	you were loving	ama-**batis**	you were loving
ama-**bat**	he, she, it was loving	ama-**bant**	they were loving

◆ The *imperfect tense sign* is **ba**. The *imperfect tense* is formed by adding the *imperfect tense endings*, **bam, bas, bat, bamus, batis, bant**, to the present stem, **ama**.

◆ *Imperfect* in Latin means *not finished*. The imperfect tense is used to describe an ongoing, repeated, habitual, or interrupted past action. It is never used to describe a single completed past action. Here are some examples of the imperfect tense in English.

I <u>was calling</u> you when the doorbell rang.   *interrupted*
I <u>used to call</u> home every week.   *repeated*

Vocabulary

Latin	English	Derivatives
aro	I plow	*arable*
clamo	I shout	*clamor*
erro	I err, wander	*erroneous*
juvo	I help	*adjutant*
laudo	I praise	*laudable*
narro	I tell	*narrator*
opto	I desire, wish	*option*
pugno	I fight	*pugnacious*
specto	I look at, I watch	*inspect*
tempto	I tempt	*temptation*

♦ The Latin word **specto** means *look at.* Sometimes an English preposition is needed to translate a Latin verb.

♦ Because the personal ending of the verb is sufficient to indicate a pronoun subject, a Latin sentence may consist of one word. Read pages 93-95 for an English grammar review and instructions on sentence labeling and diagramming.

I was fighting.	**Pugnabam.**
You were shouting.	**Clamabas.**
We are washing.	**Lavamus.**
He plows.	**Arat.**

> **Stabat Mater** is the name of an ancient Latin hymn, also called *The Dolorosa*, celebrating the emotions of Mary at the Cross. *The Dolorosa* has been set to many different lines of music, plainsong and melodic, and has been used in liturgy since at least the 14th century. Notice that the verb in *Stabat Mater* is in the imperfect tense, and precedes the subject.

Oral Drill

1. **laudabat** he was prasing
2. **laudat** he praises
3. **clamant** they shout
4. **clamabant** they were shouting
5. **juvamus** we help
6. **juvabamus** we were helping
7. **narrat** he tells
8. **narrabat** he was telling
9. **spectas** you look at
10. **spectabas** you were looking at

1. he was wandering errabat
2. they plow arant
3. she praises laudant
4. you were fighting pugnabas
5. he was desiring optabat
6. we tell narramus
7. you (p) look at spectatis
8. we were helping juvabamus
9. you err erras
10. they were praising laudabant

13

In umbra, ígitur, pugnábimus.   *Then we will fight in the shade.*

First Conjugation - Future Tense
present stem   **ama-**

Singular		Plural	
ama-**bo**	I will love	amá-**bimus**	we will love
ama-**bis**	you will love	amá-**bitis**	you will love
ama-**bit**	he, she, it will love	ama-**bunt**	they will love

♦ The *future tense sign* is **bi**. The *future tense* is formed by adding the *future tense endings*, **bo, bis, bit, bimus, bitis, bunt**, to the present stem, **ama**.

♦ The **i** in **bi** is inconsistent, being absent from the 1st person singular and changing to **u** in the 3rd person plural.

Vocabulary

adoro	I adore	*adoration*
ámbulo	I walk	*ambulance*
hábito	I live in, dwell	*habitat*
júdico	I judge, consider	*judicious*
laboro	I work	*laboratory*
líbero	I set free	*liberty*
návigo	I sail	*navigator*
óccupo	I seize	*occupy*
saluto	I greet	*salutation*
súpero	I overcome, surpass	*superior*

*Oral Drill for Lesson III is on page 110.

♦ To remember the tense signs for the imperfect and future tenses:

tense	tense sign	helping verb	vowel
future	b**i**	w**i**ll	i
imperfect	b**a**	w**a**s	a

In umbra, ígitur, pugnábimus. In August of 480 B.C., the Spartan king Leonidas with a Greek force of 7000 was holding the pass of Thermopylae against the much larger army of the invading Persian king, Xerxes I. The Greek historian Herodotus tells us of a Spartan soldier who, when told that the Persian arrows would blot out the sun, bravely replied, "So much the better, we will fight in the shade." The Latin translation is Cicero's (*Tusculan Disputations*, I,101). This phrase is the motto of the First Artillery Detachment of the United States Army.

Cicero
(Marcus Tullius Cicero) 106 BC to 43 BC
Cicero was a philosopher, politician, and Rome's greatest orator.

LESSON IV

First Conjugation - Present System

P.	S.	Present	Pl.	
1	am**o**	I love	ama**mus**	we love
2	ama**s**	you love	ama**tis**	you love
3	ama**t**	he, she, it loves	ama**nt**	they love
P.	S.	Imperfect	Pl.	
1	ama**bam**	I was loving	ama**bamus**	we were loving
2	ama**bas**	you were loving	ama**batis**	you were loving
3	ama**bat**	he, she, it was loving	ama**bant**	they were loving
P.	S.	Future	Pl.	
1	ama**bo**	I will love	amá**bimus**	we will love
2	ama**bis**	you will love	amá**bitis**	you will love
3	ama**bit**	he, she, it will love	ama**bunt**	they will love

Vocabulary Review

adoro adorare	*to adore*	**nato -are**	*to swim*
ámbulo ambulare	*to walk*	**návigo -are**	*to sail*
amo amare	*to love, like*	**óccupo -are**	*to seize*
aro arare	*to plow*	**opto -are**	*to desire, wish*
clamo clamare	*to shout*	**oro -are**	*to speak, pray*
do dare*	*to give*	**paro -are**	*to prepare*
erro -are	*to err, wander*	**porto -are**	*to carry*
hábito -are	*to live in, dwell*	**pugno -are**	*to fight*
júdico -are	*to judge, consider*	**saluto -are**	*to greet*
juvo -are*	*to help*	**servo -are**	*to guard, keep*
laboro -are	*to work*	**specto -are**	*to look at*
laudo -are	*to praise*	**sto -are***	*to stand*
lavo -are*	*to wash*	**súpero -are**	*to overcome, surpass*
líbero -are	*to set free*	**tempto -are**	*to tempt*
narro -are	*to tell*	**voco -are**	*to call*

* These verbs have irregular principal parts which will be explained in lesson 7.

The Infinitive

♦ The present, imperfect, and future tenses make up the *Present System*. All three tenses are built on the *present stem*.

♦ In the Present System there are eighteen ways to write **amo**. A Latin dictionary does not list all of these forms, but instead gives four main forms for each verb. These four main forms are called *principal parts*.

♦ The *principal parts* of a verb provide the stems needed to conjugate that verb in all of its tenses. The first two principal parts of amo are

amo   amare

♦ **Amo**, the 1st principal part, means *I love*, and is the first person singular of the present tense. It is the *entry form* of the verb in a vocabulary list or dictionary.

♦ **Amare**, the 2nd principal part, means *to love,* and has a special name, the *infinitive*. The *infinitive* of every 1st conjugation verb ends in **are**.

♦ The infinitive is used to identify the conjugation (family) a verb belongs to.

A verb whose *infinitive* ends in **are** belongs to the *1st conjugation.*

♦ The infinitive means **to** + the verb. The infinitive of **amo** is **amare** and means *to love*. From this point on, this text will use the infinitive meaning in the vocabulary lists.

♦ In a vocabulary list or dictionary entry a first conjugation verb may be written with its complete infinitive or with the infinitive ending.

amo amare   **amo -are**

♦ The *official* way to find the **stem** of a first conjugation verb is to drop the **re** from the infinitive form. It is the infinitive that contains the **stem vowel, a.**

amare   **ama/re**   stem = **ama**

♦ Say aloud the first and second principal parts of the verbs in the vocabulary review on the facing page.

Civis Romanus sum.   *I am a Roman citizen.*

Irregular Verb **sum** - Present System

sum   esse

S.	Present		Pl.
su**m**	I am	su**mus**	we are
e**s**	you are	es**tis**	you are
es**t**	he, she, it is	su**nt**	they are

S.	Imperfect		Pl.
era**m**	I was	era**mus**	we were
era**s**	you were	era**tis**	you were
era**t**	he, she, it was	era**nt**	they were

S.	Future		Pl.
er**o**	I will be	éri**mus**	we will be
eri**s**	you will be	éri**tis**	you will be
eri**t**	he, she, it will be	eru**nt**	they will be

♦ The *to be* verb, **sum**, is the most common verb in English, Latin, and many other languages. It is always irregular.

♦ The *to be* verb, **sum**, shows existence, not action. Notice that the personal endings are regular, although the infinitive, **esse**, and present stem are irregular.

♦ Forms of the *to be* verb, *am, is, are, was, were, be, being, been,* are helping verbs in English. Forms of **sum** are <u>not</u> helping verbs for the Latin tenses you have learned.

	Correct	*Incorrect*
I love, or I am loving	**Amo**	Sum amo
I was loving	**Amabam**	Eram amabam
I will love	**Amabo**	Ero amabo

*Oral Drill for Lesson V is on page 110.

♦ The *to be* verb is often a linking verb that links the subject to a noun or adjective in the predicate. When the *to be* verb is a linking verb it is similar to an equals sign.

Mary is a mother.   Mary is beautiful.
     noun   *adjective*

Mary = mother.   Mary = beautiful.

> **Civis Romanus sum** is a formula that could be used by a Roman citizen charged with a crime by a magistrate who did not have the proper authority to try him. It was a direct appeal to the emperor. It was used by St. Paul to demand that the praetors of Philippi come in person to release him. The praetors, who had illegally ordered him flogged and thrown into prison, got nervous and tried to have him released in secret (Acts 16: 35-39).

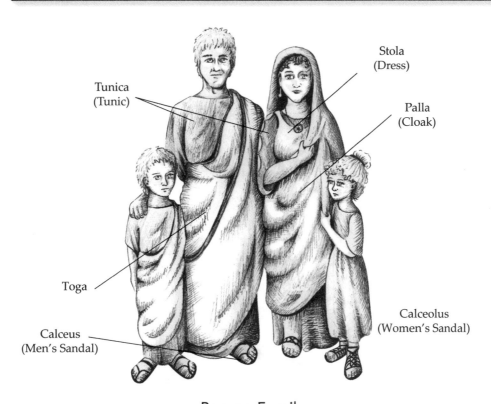

Tunica (Tunic)

Stola (Dress)

Palla (Cloak)

Toga

Calceolus (Women's Sandal)

Calceus (Men's Sandal)

Roman Family
Only Roman citizens could wear the Toga.

UNIT I REVIEW

First Conjugation - Present System

amo   amare

P.	S.	Present	Pl.	
1	am**o**	I love	ama**mus**	we love
2	ama**s**	you love	ama**tis**	you love
3	ama**t**	he, she, it loves	ama**nt**	they love
P.	S.	Imperfect	Pl.	
1	ama**bam**	I was loving	ama**bamus**	we were loving
2	ama**bas**	you were loving	ama**batis**	you were loving
3	ama**bat**	he, she, it was loving	ama**bant**	they were loving
P.	S.	Future	Pl.	
1	ama**bo**	I will love	amá**bimus**	we will love
2	ama**bis**	you will love	amá**bitis**	you will love
3	ama**bit**	he, she, it will love	ama**bunt**	they will love

Irregular Verb **sum** - Present System

sum   esse

S.	Present	Pl.	
su**m**	I am	su**mus**	we are
e**s**	you are	es**tis**	you are
es**t**	he, she, it is	su**nt**	they are
S.	Imperfect	Pl.	
era**m**	I was	era**mus**	we were
era**s**	you were	era**tis**	you were
era**t**	he, she, it was	era**nt**	they were
S.	Future	Pl.	
er**o**	I will be	éri**mus**	we will be
eri**s**	you will be	éri**tis**	you will be
eri**t**	he, she, it will be	eru**nt**	they will be

1st Conjugation Verbs

adoro -are	to adore	**nato -are**	to swim
ámbulo -are	to walk	**návigo -are**	to sail
amo -are	to love, like	**óccupo -are**	to seize
aro -are	to plow	**opto -are**	to desire, wish
clamo -are	to shout	**oro -are**	to speak, pray
do -are*	to give	**paro -are**	to prepare
erro -are	to err, wander	**porto -are**	to carry
hábito -are	to live in, dwell	**pugno -are**	to fight
júdico -are	to judge	**saluto -are**	to greet
juvo -are*	to help	**servo -are**	to guard, keep
laboro -are	to work	**specto -are**	to look at
laudo -are	to praise	**sto -are***	to stand
lavo -are*	to wash	**súpero -are**	to overcome, surpass
líbero -are	to set free	**tempto -are**	to tempt
narro -are	to tell	**voco -are**	to call

Irregular Verb

sum esse   *to be*

Latin Sayings

In choro recitémus.

Stabat Mater

Civis Romanus sum.

In umbra, ígitur, pugnábimus.

* These verbs have irregular principal parts which will be explained in lesson 7.

UNIT II INTRODUCTION

♦ The six tenses of a Latin verb are divided into two systems: the Present System and the Perfect System.

♦ The Present System has three tenses: present, imperfect, and future.

♦ The Perfect System has three tenses: perfect, pluperfect, and future perfect.

♦ The Present System is built on the present stem. The Perfect System is built on the perfect stem.

♦ A dictionary entry for a Latin verb lists four main forms called the Principal Parts.

♦ The Principal Parts provide the stems needed to conjugate a verb in all of its tenses.

♦ A verb may have regular or irregular principal parts.

Model of the Forum

UNIT II

Verbs
1st Conjugation and sum

Perfect System

The Forum Today

Errare est humanum.   *To err is human.*

Principal Parts, First Conjugation

♦ The *principal parts* are the four forms of each verb that provide the *stems* needed to conjugate that verb in all of its tenses. The principal parts of **amo** and their meanings are:

1st	2nd	3rd	4th
am **o**	am **are**	am **avi**	am **atus**[3]
I love	to love	I loved	loved

♦ To write the principal parts of regular 1st conjugation verbs, drop the **o** from the first principal part and add the regular endings **are, avi, atus**

voc **o**   voc **are**   voc **avi**   voc **atus**

clam **o**   clam **are**   clam **avi**   clam **atus**

♦ The 3rd principal part is the 1st person singular of the *perfect tense.* You will use it in the next lesson. The fourth principal part will not be used in this book.

♦ A dictionary entry for **amo** could look like this:

amo   amare   amavi   amatus

But usually a dictionary or vocabulary will shorten the entry for a regular verb and write the entry one of two ways.

amo -are   or   amo (1)

The **(1)** or the infinitive ending **are** indicate that the verb is 1st conjugation and that it has regular principal parts.

♦ Say aloud the principal parts for all of the verbs in Review Lesson VI.

♦ Some verbs have irregular principal parts. If so, the dictionary or vocabulary list will write out all of the parts. The best way to learn irregular principal parts is to say them aloud many times.

Learn these 1st conjugation verbs with irregular principal parts.

1st	2nd	3rd	4th
do	dare	dedi	datus
sto	stare	steti	status
juvo	juvare	juvi	jutus
lavo	lavare	lavi	lautus

♦ **Infinitive as subject.** The infinitive is a *verbal noun* and can be the subject of a verb as it is in this week's Latin Saying - **Errare est humanum.**

♦ **Complementary infinitive.** When an infinitive completes the action of a main verb, such as **amo, paro,** and **opto,** it is a *direct object* with a special name, the *complementary infinitive.* The infinitive may precede or follow its verb. This is *Sentence Pattern #2 on page 97.*

Amo ambulare.
I love   to walk

I love to walk.

Laborare parat.
to work   he prepares

SP   V-t   CI
He prepares to work.

Errare est humanum. This proverb has no particular author. Variations of it were common in ancient literature as they are today. One variant says that "to err is human, but to persist in error is diabolical." Another says that "to err is human, and to forgive is divine."

nunc aut numquam   *now or never*

First Conjugation - Perfect Tense

perfect stem   **amav-**

	Singular		Plural
amav**i**	I have loved	amáv**imus**	we have loved
amav**isti**	you have loved	amav**istis**	you have loved
amav**it**	he, she, it has loved	amav**erunt**	they have loved

◆   The *perfect stem* is found by dropping the personal ending **i** from the third principal part.

amo   amare   amavi   amatus

amav/i   =   amav

◆   For the Latin verb, *perfect* means *completed*. The perfect tense describes a one-time action completed in the past.

Vocabulary

cras	tomorrow	*procrastinate*
heri	yesterday	
hódie	today	
non	not	
numquam	never	
nunc	now	
saepe	often	
semper	always	
tum	then, at that time	
umquam	ever	

♦ The perfect tense is formed by adding the *perfect tense endings* to the perfect stem. The perfect tense endings are:

i	imus
isti	istis
it	erunt

♦ There are three English translations for the Latin perfect tense. For translation work any of the three are correct, although one may sound better in a particular context. For recitations use the *present perfect* meaning with the helping verbs *have* and *has*.

I loved   I have loved   I did love

Nunc aut numquam is an old saying with no known origin. It is used as a motto by many organizations, such as the Netherlands Commandos.

Oral Drill

1. **clamávimus**	1. we have judged
2. **amavi**	2. they have sailed
3. **servavistis**	3. I have worked
4. **superaverunt**	4. she has given
5. **ambulavit**	5. you (p) have prepared
6. **oravisti**	6. he has washed
7. **dederunt**	7. it has helped
8. **erravi**	8. I have told
9. **stetistis**	9. they have shouted
10. **laudavit**	10. we have fought

LESSON IX

semper fidelis *always faithful*

First Conjugation - Pluperfect Tense

perfect stem **amav-**

Singular		Plural	
amáv**eram**	I had loved	amav**eramus**	we had loved
amáv**eras**	you had loved	amav**eratis**	you had loved
amáv**erat**	he, she, it had loved	amáv**erant**	they had loved

♦ The pluperfect tense is formed by adding the *pluperfect tense endings* to the perfect stem. The pluperfect tense endings are identical to the imperfect of **sum**.

eram	eramus
eras	eratis
erat	erant

Vocabulary

accuso (1)	to accuse	*accusation*
celo (1)	to hide	*conceal*
dúbito (1)	to doubt	*dubious*
muto (1)	to change	*mutate*
nego (1)	to deny	*negative*
perturbo (1)	to disturb	*perturb*
puto (1)	to think	*computer*
rogo (1)	to ask	*interrogative*
spero (1)	to hope	*despair*
volo (1)	to fly	*volley, volatile*

*Oral Drill for Lesson IX is on page 111.

♦ The pluperfect tense describes a past action completed prior to another past action.

Caesar *had conquered* the Gauls before he crossed the Rubicon.

I *had finished* my homework when the doorbell rang.

♦ The pluperfect tense is translated into English by the helping verb **had**.

Semper fidelis is the well-known motto of the United States Marine Corps. Marines often use the short form "Semper Fi" as a salutation to one another.

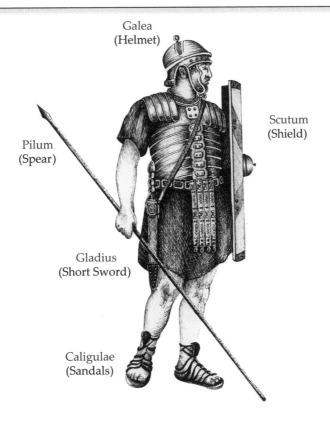

Galea
(Helmet)

Scutum
(Shield)

Pilum
(Spear)

Gladius
(Short Sword)

Caligulae
(Sandals)

Roman Legionary

LESSON X

Fortes fortuna juvat. *Fortune aids the brave.*

First Conjugation - Future Perfect Tense

perfect stem **amav-**

Singular		Plural	
amáv **ero**	I will have loved	amav **érimus**	we will have loved
amáv **eris**	you will have loved	amav **éritis**	you will have loved
amáv **erit**	hsi will have loved	amáv **erint**	they will have loved

♦ The *future perfect tense* is formed by adding the *future perfect tense endings* to the perfect stem. The future perfect tense endings are the same as the future of **sum**, excepting the 3rd person plural.

ero	erimus
eris	eritis
erit	<u>erint</u>

Vocabulary

appello (1)	to address	*appeal*
creo (1)	to create	*create*
culpo (1)	to blame	*culprit, culpable*
delecto (1)	to delight, please	*delectable*
demonstro (1)	to show, point out	*demonstrate*
exploro (1)	to explore	*explore*
exspecto (1)	to wait for, expect	*expect*
núntio (1)	to report	*announce*
oppugno (1)	to attack	*pugnacious*
vúlnero (1)	to wound	*vulnerable*

*Oral Drill for Lesson X is on page 111.

♦ The future perfect tense describes a future action that will be completed prior to another future action.

By the end of this course <u>you will have learned</u> two conjugations and all five declensions.

> **Fortes fortuna juvat.** This phrase was coined by the Roman playwright Terence and adapted by Vergil in the *Aeneid*, Book X, line 284. It is currently used as the motto of the 3rd Regiment of the U.S. Marine Corps.

Vergil
(Publius Vergilius Maro) 70 -19 BC
The author of Rome's great epic poem, the *Aeneid*

Ora et labora. *Pray and work.*

Irregular Verb **sum**
Perfect System

perfect stem **fu-**

S.	Perfect		Pl.	
fu**i**	I have been	fú**imus**	we have been
fu**isti**	you have been	fu**istis**	you have been
fu**it**	he, she, it has been	fu**erunt**	they have been

S.	Pluperfect		Pl.	
fú**eram**	I had been	fu**eramus**	we had been
fú**eras**	you had been	fu**eratis**	you had been
fú**erat**	he, she, it had been	fú**erant**	they had been

S.	Future Perfect		Pl.	
fú**ero**	I will have been	fu**érimus**	we will have been
fú**eris**	you will have been	fu**éritis**	you will have been
fú**erit**	he, she, it will have been	fú**erint**	they will have been

♦ The principal parts of **sum** are irregular. The perfect stem of **sum** is **fu**.

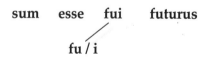

sum   esse   fui   futurus

fu / i

♦ The perfect system endings of **sum** are regular.

Ora et labora. St. Benedict has been called one of the founders of Western Civilization, and even the *Father of Europe*. In 530 A.D., while the barbarians were fighting over Rome, St. Benedict and a small band of monks established a monastery at Monte Cassino, eighty-five miles southeast of Rome. The monasteries were oases of peace and learning during these dark ages, the cells that preserved the Christian faith and civilization until the ravages of the barbarians ended. St. Benedict's famous Rule for the life of monks became the basis for all monastic life which spread across Europe in the following centuries. *Ora et labora* is a summary of the Rule of St. Benedict and is a good rule for our lives, too.

Oral Drill

1. **fúimus**	1. I have been
2. **fueramus**	2. you had been
3. **fuérimus**	3. we have been
4. **fui**	4. she has been
5. **fúeram**	5. they have been
6. **fuerunt**	6. you (p) will have been
7. **fúerint**	7. he will have been
8. **fúerat**	8. we had been
9. **fúerit**	9. I had been
10. **fuisti**	10. they will have been

UNIT II REVIEW

Perfect System 1st Conjugation - **amo**

perfect stem **amav-**

S.	Perfect	Pl.	
amav**i**	I have loved	amáv**imus**	we have loved
amav**isti**	you have loved	amav**istis**	you have loved
amav**it**	he, she, it has loved	amav**erunt**	they have loved
S.	Pluperfect	Pl.	
amáv**eram**	I had loved	amav**eramus**	we had loved
amáv**eras**	you had loved	amav**eratis**	you had loved
amáv**erat**	he, she, it had loved	amáv**erant**	they had loved
S.	Future Perfect	Pl.	
amáv**ero**	I will have loved	amav**érimus**	we will have loved
amáv**eris**	you will have loved	amav**éritis**	you will have loved
amáv**erit**	he, she, it will have loved	amáv**erint**	they will have loved

Perfect System - Irregular Verb **sum**

perfect stem **fu-**

S.	Perfect	Pl.	
fu**i**	I have been	fú**imus**	we have been
fu**isti**	you have been	fu**istis**	you have been
fu**it**	he, she, it has been	fu**erunt**	they have been
S.	Pluperfect	Pl.	
fú**eram**	I had been	fu**eramus**	we had been
fú**eras**	you had been	fu**eratis**	you had been
fú**erat**	he, she, it had been	fú**erant**	they had been
S.	Future Perfect	Pl.	
fú**ero**	I will have been	fu**érimus**	we will have been
fú**eris**	you will have been	fu**éritis**	you will have been
fú**erit**	he, she, it will have been	fú**erint**	they will have been

Verbs

accuso (1)	*to accuse*	**muto (1)**	*to change*
appello (1)	*to address*	**nego (1)**	*to deny*
celo (1)	*to hide*	**núntio (1)**	*to report*
creo (1)	*to create*	**oppugno (1)**	*to attack*
culpo (1)	*to blame*	**perturbo (1)**	*to disturb*
delecto (1)	*to delight, please*	**puto (1)**	*to think*
demonstro (1)	*to show, point out*	**rogo (1)**	*to ask*
dúbito (1)	*to doubt*	**spero (1)**	*to hope*
exploro (1)	*to explore*	**volo (1)**	*to fly*
exspecto (1)	*to wait for, expect*	**vúlnero (1)**	*to wound*

Principal Parts

1st	2nd	3rd	4th
am o	**am are**	**am avi**	**am atus**
I love	*to love*	*I loved*	*loved*
do	**dare**	**dedi**	**datus**
sto	**stare**	**steti**	**status**
juvo	**juvare**	**juvi**	**jutus**
lavo	**lavare**	**lavi**	**lautus**
sum	**esse**	**fui**	**futurus**

Adverbs

cras	*tomorrow*	**nunc**	*now*
heri	*yesterday*	**saepe**	*often*
hódie	*today*	**semper**	*always*
non	*not*	**tum**	*then, at that time*
numquam	*never*	**umquam**	*ever*

Latin Sayings

Ora et labora.	**nunc aut numquam**
semper fidelis	**Fortes fortuna juvat.**
Errare est humanum.	

UNITS I and II REVIEW

First Conjugation - Indicative Active
amo amare amavi amatus

present stem **ama -**

Present	
am**o**	ama**mus**
ama**s**	ama**tis**
ama**t**	ama**nt**

Imperfect	
ama**bam**	ama**bamus**
ama**bas**	ama**batis**
ama**bat**	ama**bant**

Future	
ama**bo**	amá**bimus**
ama**bis**	amá**bitis**
ama**bit**	ama**bunt**

perfect stem **amav -**

Perfect	
amav**i**	amáv**imus**
amav**isti**	amav**istis**
amav**it**	amav**erunt**

Pluperfect	
amáv**eram**	amav**eramus**
amáv**eras**	amav**eratis**
amáv**erat**	amáv**erant**

Future Perfect	
amáv**ero**	amav**érimus**
amáv**eris**	amav**éritis**
amáv**erit**	amáv**erint**

Sum - Indicative Active
sum esse fui futurus

present stem **--**

Present	
su**m**	su**mus**
e**s**	es**tis**
es**t**	su**nt**

Imperfect	
era**m**	era**mus**
era**s**	era**tis**
era**t**	era**nt**

Future	
er**o**	éri**mus**
eri**s**	éri**tis**
eri**t**	eru**nt**

perfect stem **fu-**

Perfect	
fu**i**	fú**imus**
fu**isti**	fu**istis**
fu**it**	fu**erunt**

Pluperfect	
fú**eram**	fu**eramus**
fú**eras**	fu**eratis**
fú**erat**	fú**erant**

Future Perfect	
fú**ero**	fu**érimus**
fú**eris**	fu**éritis**
fú**erit**	fú**erint**

Verbs

accuso	*to accuse*	**hábito**	*to live in, dwell*	**paro**	*to prepare*
adoro	*to adore*	**júdico**	*to judge*	**perturbo**	*to disturb*
ámbulo	*to walk*	**juvo**	*to help*	**porto**	*to carry*
amo	*to love, like*	**laboro**	*to work*	**pugno**	*to fight*
appello	*to address*	**laudo**	*to praise*	**puto**	*to think*
aro	*to plow*	**lavo**	*to wash*	**rogo**	*to ask*
celo	*to hide*	**líbero**	*to set free*	**saluto**	*to greet*
clamo	*to shout*	**muto**	*to change*	**servo**	*to guard, keep*
creo	*to create*	**narro**	*to tell*	**specto**	*to look at*
culpo	*to blame*	**nato**	*to swim*	**spero**	*to hope*
delecto	*to delight, please*	**návigo**	*to sail*	**sto**	*to stand*
demonstro	*to show, point out*	**nego**	*to deny*	**súpero**	*to overcome, surpass*
do	*to give*	**núntio**	*to report*	**tempto**	*to tempt*
dúbito	*to doubt*	**óccupo**	*to seize*	**voco**	*to call*
erro	*to err, wander*	**oppugno**	*to attack*	**volo**	*to fly*
exploro	*to explore*	**opto**	*to desire, wish*	**vúlnero**	*to wound*
exspecto	*to wait for, expect*	**oro**	*to speak, pray*	**sum**	*to be*

Adverbs

cras	*tomorrow*	**nunc**	*now*
heri	*yesterday*	**saepe**	*often*
hódie	*today*	**semper**	*always*
non	*not*	**tum**	*then, at that time*
numquam	*never*	**umquam**	*ever*

Latin Sayings

Ora et labora.
Stabat Mater
In umbra, ígitur, pugnábimus.
In choro recitémus.
Errare est humanum.

Civis Romanus sum.
nunc aut numquam
semper fidelis
Fortes fortuna juvat.

UNIT III INTRODUCTION

♦ Just as verbs are divided into four families called conjugations, nouns are grouped into five families called *declensions*.

♦ There are four attributes of nouns:

declension	1st, 2nd, 3rd, 4th, 5th
gender	masculine, feminine, neuter
number	singular and plural
case	nominative, genitive, dative, accusative, ablative

♦ Nouns that name male or female persons, such as *father* or *queen,* are masculine or feminine and have *natural* (real) *gender.* Nouns that name non-living things have *grammatical gender* and are identified as masculine, feminine, or neuter.

♦ Case refers to the job (function) of a noun in a sentence. (See the Appendix, pages 102-104) Learn these quick uses for the Latin cases.

nominative	the *subject* case	the rose
genitive	the *possessive* or *of* case	of the rose
dative	the *indirect object* or *to/for* case	to the rose
accusative	the *direct object* case	the rose
ablative	the *in/by/with/from* case	in the rose

♦ The 1st and 2nd declension nouns and adjectives are similar and will be studied together. The 3rd-5th Declensions will be studied in Unit 4.

♦ In Latin vocabulary lists and dictionaries, the nominative singular form is followed by the genitive singular ending and the gender. This is a listing for *rose* in a Latin dictionary or vocabulary list.

rosa, ae *f.* rose

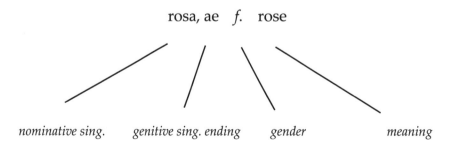

nominative sing.   *genitive sing. ending*   *gender*   *meaning*

UNIT III
1st and 2nd Declension Nouns and Adjectives

A Relief from the Arch of Titus

Spoils taken from the Temple of Jerusalem in the Jewish War—depicted on the Arch of Titus on the Via Sacra in the Forum Romanum. The arch, commemorating the sack of Jerusalem in AD 70, clearly shows the Roman soldiers carrying the seven-candlestick menorah in a victory procession. For Americans today this is one of the most meaningful and poignant sights in the ancient Forum.

Roma Aeterna   *Eternal Rome*

First Declension

Case	Singular	Ending	Plural	Ending
nominative	mens**a**	-a	mens**ae**	-ae
genitive	mens**ae**	-ae	mens**arum**	-arum
dative	mens**ae**	-ae	mens**is**	-is
accusative	mens**am**	-am	mens**as**	-as
ablative	mens**ā**	-ā	mens**is**	-is

◆ **Mensa** is the model noun chosen to illustrate the *1st Declension*. The stem of **mensa** is **mens**. Drop the nominative singular ending **a** to find the stem.[4] To *decline* a noun, add the *case endings* to the stem.

◆ The ablative singular ending of 1st declension nouns will be marked with a *macron* in this text to distinguish it from the nominative singular ending.[5]

◆ In English, the words **the, a,** and **an** are called *articles*. There are no *articles* in Latin. **Mensa** may be translated three ways: **table, a table, the table.**

◆ All nouns whose *genitive singular* ends in **ae** belong to the 1st Declension.

Vocabulary

Latin	Gender	English	Derivative
agrícola -ae	*m.*	farmer	*agriculture*
Itália -ae	*f.*	Italy	
Maria -ae	*f.*	Mary	
mensa -ae	*f.*	table	*mesa*
nauta -ae	*m.*	sailor	*nautical*
poeta -ae	*m.*	poet	
puella -ae	*f.*	girl	
regina -ae	*f.*	queen	
Roma -ae	*f.*	Rome	
terra -ae	*f.*	earth, land	*territory*

*Oral Drill for Lesson XIV is on page 112.

♦ Every Latin noun has *gender*. There are three genders: *masculine, feminine and neuter,* identified by the abbreviations **m., f., n.**

♦ 1st declension nouns are usually *feminine,* even when they name non-living things like **mensa, Italia, terra** and **Roma.**

♦ Some nouns have *natural gender* in addition to their *grammar* gender. **Maria, puella,** and **regina** name female persons so they are feminine by nature.

♦ However, **nauta, agricola,** and **poeta** are masculine by nature because they name male persons. (In the Roman world these occupations were always male.) If the natural gender and grammar gender are different, natural gender always wins.

♦ Here are two gender rules to remember with their abbreviations.
  1) NG. Natural Gender. Nouns that name male persons are masculine and nouns that name female persons are feminine. Natural gender *trumps* all other gender rules.
  2) 1D F. 1st declension nouns are usually feminine.

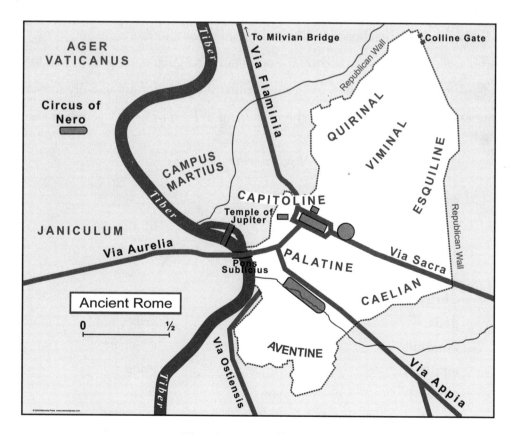

The Seven Hills of Rome

41

LESSON XV

Anno Dómini (A.D.)   *In the year of our Lord*

Second Declension Masculine

Case	Singular	Ending	Plural	Ending
nominative	serv**us**	-us	serv**i**	-i
genitive	serv**i**	-i	serv**orum**	-orum
dative	serv**o**	-o	serv**is**	-is
accusative	serv**um**	-um	serv**os**	-os
ablative	serv**o**	-o	serv**is**	-is

♦ **Servus** is the model noun chosen to illustrate *2nd Declension* nouns ending in **us**.

♦ The stem is **serv**. For these nouns, drop the nominative singular ending **us** to find the stem.[4]

♦ 2nd declension nouns that end in **us** in the nominative singular are usually **masculine**.

♦ **Deus** and **Dominus** are capitalized when referring to *Jesus* or *God*. Use lower case when referring to pagan gods.

Vocabulary

Latin	Gender	English	Derivative
agnus -i	*m.*	lamb	*St. Agnes*
amicus -i	*m.*	friend	*amicable*
annus -i	*m.*	year	*annual*
Christus -i	*m.*	Christ	
deus -i	*m.*	god	*deity*
dóminus -i	*m.*	lord, master	*dominate*
equus -i	*m.*	horse	*equine*
fílius -i	*m.*	son	*filial*
mundus -i	*m.*	world, mankind	*mundane*
servus -i	*m.*	slave, servant	*servile*

♦ The subject of a verb is in the nominative case. To form a plural subject, use the plural nominative case ending, **i** for 2nd decl. **us** nouns, and **ae** for 1st declension nouns.

♦ Here is a third gender rule.
   (3) **2D us M**: 2nd declension **us** nouns are usually masculine.

♦ English words that show their 1st/2nd declension origin by retaining the Latin plural endings are:

alumna, alumnae	*formula, formulae*	*fungus, fungi*
alumnus, alumni	*cactus, cacti*	

Anno Dómini. The dating system based on the birth of Christ was developed in the Middle Ages. *B.C.* stands for the English *Before Christ. A.D.* stands for the Latin **Anno Dómini**, which means *in the year of Our Lord. A.D.* refers to a year following the birth of Christ, and does not mean *after death.*

Oral Drill - Nominative Case

1.	**annus**	1.	horse
2.	**mundus**	2.	son
3.	**amici**	3.	gods
4.	**equi**	4.	lambs
5.	**agnus**	5.	friend
6.	**fílii**	6.	worlds
7.	**servi**	7.	years
8.	**dómini**	8.	servant
9.	**Christus**	9.	lord
10.	**deus**	10.	Christ

ante bellum   *before the war*

Second Declension Neuter

Case	Singular	Ending	Plural	Ending
nominative	bell**um**	-um	bell**a**	-a
genitive	bell**i**	-i	bell**orum**	-orum
dative	bell**o**	-o	bell**is**	-is
accusative	bell**um**	-um	bell**a**	-a
ablative	bell**o**	-o	bell**is**	-is

♦ **Bellum** is the model noun chosen to illustrate 2nd declension nouns ending in **um**. The stem is **bell**. For these nouns, drop the nominative singular ending **um** to find the stem.[4]

♦ The 2nd declension has two subgroups: 1) nouns that end in **us** in the nominative singular and are usually masculine 2) nouns that end in **um** in the nominative singular and are **neuter** (*n*).

All nouns whose genitive singular ends in **i** belong to the 2nd Declension.

Vocabulary

bellum -i	*n.*	war	*bellicose*
caelum -i	*n.*[6]	sky, heaven	*celestial*
débitum -i	*n.*	debt, sin	*debit*
donum -i	*n.*	gift	*donation*
forum -i	*n.*	forum, marketplace	*forum*
óppidum -i	*n.*	town	
regnum -i	*n.*	kingdom	*reign*
saxum -i	*n.*	rock	
templum -i	*n.*	temple	
verbum -i	*n.*	word	*verb, verbal*

♦ There are neuter nouns in the 2nd, 3rd, and 4th declensions. All neuter nouns obey the *neuter rule*:

> **the nominative and accusative case forms are identical**
> **the nominative and accusative plural case ending is -a**

♦ Here is a fourth gender rule.
(4) **2D um N**: 2nd declension nouns that end in **um** are neuter.

♦ As you learn the 5 declensions you will see that a particular ending can indicate different cases in different declensions. The letter **a** is the nominative singular ending in the 1st declension, but it is the nominative and accusative plural ending in the 2nd declension neuter.

♦ English words that show their 2nd declension neuter origin by retaining the Latin plural endings are:

datum, data   *medium, media*   *bacterium, bacteria*
curriculum, curricula   *stratum, strata*   *memorandum, memoranda*

> **Ante bellum** refers to the unique culture of a landed aristocracy that existed in the American South before the Civil War.

Oral Drill - Nominative Case

1. **poeta**		1. gift
2. **nauta**		2. gifts
3. **bella**		3. wars
4. **verba**		4. war
5. **debita**		5. towns
6. **dona**		6. town
7. **puella**		7. kingdom
8. **óppida**		8. kingdoms
9. **terra**		9. word
10. **saxa**		10. words

First and Second Declensions

Case	1st Declension S.	1st Declension Pl.	2nd Declension Masculine S.	2nd Declension Masculine Pl.	2nd Declension Neuter S.	2nd Declension Neuter Pl.
nom.	mens**a**	mens**ae**	serv**us**	serv**i**	bell**um**	bell**a**
gen.	mens**ae**	mens**arum**	serv**i**	serv**orum**	bell**i**	bell**orum**
dat.	mens**ae**	mens**is**	serv**o**	serv**is**	bell**o**	bell**is**
acc.	mens**am**	mens**as**	serv**um**	serv**os**	bell**um**	bell**a**
abl.	mens**ā**	mens**is**	serv**o**	serv**is**	bell**o**	bell**is**

♦ The 1st and 2nd declensions can be considered a unit because they include all three genders and have similar case endings.

Vocabulary Review

agnus -i m.	*lamb*		**Maria -ae f.**	*Mary*
agrícola -ae m.	*farmer*		**mensa -ae f.**	*table*
amicus -i m.	*friend*		**mundus -i m.**	*world, mankind*
annus -i m.	*year*		**nauta -ae m.**	*sailor*
bellum -i n.	*war*		**óppidum -i n.**	*town*
caelum -i n.	*sky, heaven*		**poeta -ae m.**	*poet*
Christus -i m.	*Christ*		**puella -ae f.**	*girl*
débitum -i n.	*debt, sin*		**regina -ae f.**	*queen*
deus -i m.	*god*		**regnum -i n.**	*kingdom*
dóminus -i m.	*lord, master*		**Roma -ae f.**	*Rome*
donum -i n.	*gift*		**saxum -i n.**	*rock*
equus -i m.	*horse*		**servus -i m.**	*slave, servant*
fílius -i m.	*son*		**templum -i n.**	*temple*
forum -i n.	*forum, marketplace*		**terra -ae f.**	*earth, land*
Itália -ae f.	*Italy*		**verbum -i n.**	*word*

◆ Because the nominative singular is variable in most declensions, the genitive singular is used to classify nouns.

> If the genitive singular ends in **-ae** the noun is 1st declension.
> If the genitive singular ends in **-i** the noun is 2nd declension.

◆ English names often correspond to the Latin masculine and feminine endings.
   Julius/Julia   *Cornelius/Cornelia*   *Marius/Maria*   *Marcus/Marcia*

◆ **Subject-verb Agreement**. If the subject of the verb is a noun, the 3rd person form of the verb is used. The subject and verb must agree in person and number. A singular subject takes a singular verb; a plural subject takes a plural verb. This is *Sentence Pattern #1* on pages 95-96.

Singular:
Servus laborat. *The servant (he) works.*

Plural:
Servi laborant. *The servants (they) work.*

Oral Drill - Nominative Case

1. **terrae**	1. kingdoms
2. **anni**	2. world
3. **regina**	3. temples
4. **verba**	4. poets
5. **equus**	5. friends
6. **nautae**	6. debts
7. **saxum**	7. heaven
8. **agnus**	8. wars
9. **filii**	9. girl
10. **dona**	10. servants

Mater Itáliae Roma.   *The mother of Italy, Rome.*

First and Second Declension Adjectives

Case	Singular			Plural		
	M.	F.	N.	M.	F.	N.
nom.	bon us	bon a	bon um	bon i	bon ae	bon a
gen.	bon i	bon ae	bon i	bon orum	bon arum	bon orum
dat.	bon o	bon ae	bon o	bon is	bon is	bon is
acc.	bon um	bon am	bon um	bon os	bon as	bon a
abl.	bon o	bon ā	bon o	bon is	bon is	bon is

♦ An adjective modifies or describes a noun or pronoun. In Latin there are adjectives that are declined in all three genders with endings identical to the nouns of the 1st and 2nd declensions. They are called *1st/2nd Declension Adjectives.*

♦ In dictionary form, the adjective is given in its masculine form, followed by the feminine and neuter nominative singular endings.

Vocabulary

aeternus -a -um	eternal, everlasting	*eternity*
altus -a -um	high, deep	*altitude*
bonus -a -um	good	*bonus*
latus -a -um	wide, broad	*latitude*
magnus -a -um	great, large	*magnify*
malus -a -um	bad	*malice*
multus -a -um	much (pl. many)	*multitude*
novus -a -um	new	*novelty, novel*
parvus -a -um	small	
sanctus -a -um	sacred, holy	*sanctify*

*Oral Drill for Lesson XVIII is on page 112.

♦ In Latin, adjectives may precede or follow their nouns. Though not a strict rule, adjectives of quantity or size often precede nouns, and adjectives of quality often follow nouns. Some adjectives such as *magnus, altus,* and *latus* can refer to either quantity or quality depending on the context.

♦ In Latin, an adjective must agree with its noun in gender, number, and case,

puell**a** bon**a**	serv**us** bon**us**	oppid**um** bon**um**
good girl	*good servant*	*good town*

but not declension. The three 1st declension masculine nouns, **agricola**, **poeta**, and **nauta**, are modified by the 2nd declension masculine adjective forms.

agricol**a** bon**us**	agricol**ae** bon**i**
good farmer	*good farmers*

Mater Italiae Roma. Through conquest, the language and culture of Rome united Italy and the whole Mediterranean world, and thus Rome gave birth not only to Italy but to Western Civilization. This saying is from the Roman historian, Florus.

Quattuor anni témpora   *The four seasons of the year*

Numbers 1 - 10

	Cardinal		Ordinal	
I	**unus -a -um**	one	**primus -a -um**	first
II	**duo**	two	**secundus -a -um**	second
III	**tres**	three	**tértius -a -um**	third
IV	**quattuor**	four	**quartus -a -um**	fourth
V	**quinque**	five	**quintus -a -um**	fifth
VI	**sex**	six	**sextus -a -um**	sixth
VII	**septem**	seven	**séptimus -a -um**	seventh
VIII	**octo**	eight	**octavus -a -um**	eighth
IX	**novem**	nine	**nonus -a -um**	ninth
X	**decem**	ten	**décimus -a -um**	tenth

♦ **Cardinal** means most important. Cardinal numbers are counting numbers. The cardinal numbers are a special type of adjective. The numbers **four-ten** are indeclinable. **Unus, duo,** and **tres** are declinable but will not be declined in this text because they have irregularities in some cases.[7]

♦ **Ordinal** numbers order things in a series. The ordinal numbers are regular 1st-2nd declension adjectives.

♦ The *to be* verb, **sum**, shows existence not action. It is usually a *linking verb*, and <u>never</u> takes a direct object.

♦ A sentence is divided into two main parts: the *subject* and the *predicate*. The subject is **who** or **what** the sentence is about. The predicate contains the verb and tells something about the subject.

♦ A *predicate adjective* is an adjective that follows a linking verb, describes the subject, and is in the nominative case. See *Sentence Pattern #3*, page 98.

Puella est bona.   **Puellae sunt bonae.**
The girl is good.   *The girls are good.*

♦ A *predicate nominative* is a noun that follows a linking verb, renames the subject, and is in the nominative case. See *Sentence Pattern #4*, page 98.

Marcus est agrícola.   **Christus est Dóminus.**   **Puellae erunt reginae.**
Mark is a farmer.   Christ is Lord.   The girls will be queens.

Quattuor anni témpora   The Romans recognized four seasons, as we do.

Oral Drill - Nominative Case

1. **septem regna** | 1. eight horses
2. **primus fílius** | 2. the ninth girl
3. **novem agni** | 3. six sailors
4. **secundum verbum** | 4. the eighth queen
5. **quinque dona** | 5. the third town
6. **decem anni** | 6. five rocks
7. **décimus annus** | 7. the seventh word
8. **sexta puella** | 8. the fourth farmer
9. **tértium óppidum** | 9. a sixth son
10. **nona regina** | 10. four friends

LESSON XX

UNIT III REVIEW

First and Second Declension Nouns

Case	1st Declension		2nd Declension Masculine		2nd Declension Neuter	
	S.	Pl.	S.	Pl.	S.	Pl.
nom.	mens**a**	mens**ae**	serv**us**	serv**i**	bell**um**	bell**a**
gen.	mens**ae**	mens**arum**	serv**i**	serv**orum**	bell**i**	bell**orum**
dat.	mens**ae**	mens**is**	serv**o**	serv**is**	bell**o**	bell**is**
acc.	mens**am**	mens**as**	serv**um**	serv**os**	bell**um**	bell**a**
abl.	mens**ā**	mens**is**	serv**o**	serv**is**	bell**o**	bell**is**

First and Second Declension Adjectives

Case	Singular			Plural		
	M.	F.	N.	M.	F.	N.
nom.	bon**us**	bon**a**	bon**um**	bon**i**	bon**ae**	bon**a**
gen.	bon**i**	bon**ae**	bon**i**	bon**orum**	bon**arum**	bon**orum**
dat.	bon**o**	bon**ae**	bon**o**	bon**is**	bon**is**	bon**is**
acc.	bon**um**	bon**am**	bon**um**	bon**os**	bon**as**	bon**a**
abl.	bon**o**	bon**ā**	bon**o**	bon**is**	bon**is**	bon**is**

Numbers

Roman Numerals	Cardinal		Ordinal	
I	**unus -a -um**	one	**primus -a -um**	first
II	**duo**	two	**secundus -a -um**	second
III	**tres**	three	**tértius -a -um**	third
IV	**quattuor**	four	**quartus -a -um**	fourth
V	**quinque**	five	**quintus -a -um**	fifth
VI	**sex**	six	**sextus -a -um**	sixth
VII	**septem**	seven	**séptimus -a -um**	seventh
VIII	**octo**	eight	**octavus -a -um**	eighth
IX	**novem**	nine	**nonus -a -um**	ninth
X	**decem**	ten	**décimus -a -um**	tenth

Vocabulary Review

aeternus -a -um	*eternal everlasting*	**equus -i m.**	*horse*	**parvus -a -um**	*small*
agnus -i m.	*lamb*	**fílius -i m.**	*son*	**poeta -ae m.**	*poet*
agrícola -ae m.	*farmer*	**forum -i n.**	*forum, marketplace*	**puella -ae f.**	*girl*
altus -a -um	*high, deep*	**Itália -ae f.**	*Italy*	**regina -ae f.**	*queen*
amicus -i m.	*friend*	**latus -a -um**	*wide, broad*	**regnum -i n.**	*kingdom*
annus -i m.	*year*	**magnus -a -um**	*great, large*	**Roma -ae f.**	*Rome*
bellum -i n.	*war*	**malus -a -um**	*bad*	**sanctus -a -um**	*sacred, holy*
bonus -a -um	*good*	**Maria -ae f.**	*Mary*	**saxum -i n.**	*rock*
caelum -i n.	*sky, heaven*	**mensa -ae f.**	*table*	**servus -i m.**	*slave, servant*
Christus -i m.	*Christ*	**multus -a -um**	*much, many*	**templum -i n.**	*temple*
débitum -i n.	*debt, sin*	**mundus -i m.**	*world, mankind*	**terra -ae f.**	*earth, land*
deus -i m.	*god*	**nauta -ae m.**	*sailor*	**verbum -i n.**	*word*
dóminus -i m.	*lord, master*	**novus -a -um**	*new*		
donum -i n.	*gift*	**óppidum -i n.**	*town*		

Grammar Review

♦ Four gender rules: (1) **NG** (2) **1D F** (3) **2D us M** (4) **2D um N**

♦ The neuter rule. For every neuter noun the nominative and accusative case forms are identical, and the nominative and accusative plural ending is **-a**.

♦ A verb agrees with its subject in person and number.

♦ An adjective agrees with its noun in gender, number, and case, and may precede or follow its noun.

♦ A noun or adjective in the predicate that follows a linking verb and renames or describes the subject is in the nominative case and is called a predicate nominative or a predicate adjective.

♦ The genitive singular of a 1st declension noun is **-ae**, and of a 2nd declension noun is **-i**.

Latin Sayings

Roma Aeterna   **Anno Dómini (A.D.)**   **ante bellum**
Quattuor anni témpora   **Mater Italiae Roma**

UNIT IV INTRODUCTION

♦ There are five declensions in Latin. Declensions 1 and 2 are similar and were studied in Unit III.

♦ Declensions 3-5 will be studied in this unit.

♦ The 3rd declension is the largest declension. 3rd declension nouns are more challenging than 1st and 2nd declension nouns.

♦ 3rd declension nouns may change spelling significantly from the nominative to the genitive. The genitive form must be written out in full.

lex legis   flumen fluminis

♦ The 3rd declension has all three genders, but masculine and feminine nouns have identical case endings. Thus, there are only two models to learn in the 3rd declension.[8]

1) masculine/feminine   2) neuter

♦ There are no gender-specific nominative endings in the 3rd declension. The gender of each noun must be memorized individually.

♦ There are 3rd declension adjectives but they will not be studied in this text.

♦ The 4th and 5th declensions have few nouns and no adjectives. Most 4th declension nouns are masculine; most 5th declension nouns are feminine.

UNIT IV
NOUNS
3RD, 4TH, AND 5TH DECLENSIONS

Colosseum today (top), model (below)

alma mater   *nurturing mother*

Third Declension   Masculine and Feminine

stem **patr-**

Case	Singular	Ending	Plural	Ending
nom.	pater	-	patr**es**	**-es**
gen.	patr**is**	**-is**	patr**um**	**-um**
dat.	patr**i**	**-i**	pátr**ibus**	**-ibus**
acc.	patr**em**	**-em**	patr**es**	**-es**
abl.	patr**e**	**-e**	pátr**ibus**	**-ibus**

♦ Masculine and feminine nouns of the *3rd Declension* have the same case endings.

♦ There is no characteristic nominative singular ending in the 3rd declension. The chart has a dash to show that the nominative singular form is variable.

♦ The change in spelling from the nominative to the genitive form can be significant. In a dictionary entry the genitive form must be written out in full as shown below.

♦ The nominative singular cannot be used to find the stem. To find the stem of a 3rd declension noun, drop the genitive singular ending, **is**.

Vocabulary

dux ducis	*m.*	leader	*duke*
frater fratris	*m.*	brother	*fraternity*
mater matris	*f.*	mother	*maternity*
miles mílitis	*m.*	soldier	*military*
pater patris	*m.*	father	*patrician*
rex regis	*m.*	king	*regal*
soror sororis	*f.*	sister	*sorority*

◆ Because the nominative singular ending is variable and doesn't necessarily provide the stem, the generalization for Latin nouns of all declensions is:

> **Memorize the genitive singular of every Latin noun carefully. The genitive singular (1) identifies the declension of the noun and (2) provides the stem.**

◆ The 3rd declension has all three genders. The nouns in this list all have natural gender.

◆ 3rd declension nouns can be modified by 1st/2nd declension adjectives. The adjective agrees with its noun in gender, number, and case, but not declension.

good father	**pater bonus**	*good fathers*	**patres boni**
good mother	**mater bona**	*good mothers*	**matres bonae**

Alma mater refers to the school one graduates from. John Cardinal Newman said a university should be an alma mater, "knowing her children one by one, not a foundry, or a mint or a treadmill."

Oral Drill - Nominative Case

1.	**mílites**	1.	leaders
2.	**sorores**	2.	king
3.	**rex**	3.	sisters
4.	**fratres**	4.	soldier
5.	**dux**	5.	soldiers
6.	**mater**	6.	brother
7.	**fílii**	7.	kings
8.	**soror**	8.	father
9.	**bella**	9.	girls
10.	**patres**	10.	leader

57

Pax Romana *The Roman Peace*

Third Declension   Masculine and Feminine

stem **leg-**

Case	Singular	Ending	Plural	Ending
nom.	lex	-	leg**es**	-es
gen.	leg**is**	-is	leg**um**	-um
dat.	leg**i**	-i	lég**ibus**	-ibus
acc.	leg**em**	-em	leg**es**	-es
abl.	leg**e**	-e	lég**ibus**	-ibus

♦ The 3rd declension nouns in the previous lesson had natural gender. The nouns in this lesson have grammatical gender. The case endings are the same.

♦ The grammatical gender of 3rd declension nouns must be memorized individually. There are no characteristic endings such as **a, us,** or **um** to indicate the gender of a 3rd declension noun.

Vocabulary

canis canis	*m. or f.*	dog	*canine*
crux crucis	*f.*	cross	*crucify*
lex legis	*f.*	law	*legal*
lux lucis	*f.*	light	*lucid, Lucifer*
mos moris	*m.*	custom	*moral*
panis panis	*m.*	bread	*companion*
pax pacis	*f.*	peace	*pacific*
pes pedis	*m.*	foot	*pedal*
sol solis	*m.*	sun	*solar*
vox vocis	*f.*	voice	*vocal*

*Oral Drill for Lesson XXII is on page 113.

♦ As you learn more 3rd declension nouns you will begin to see patterns that will help you remember the gender of each noun. For instance, 3rd declension nouns that end in **x** are usually feminine. Remember, however, that natural gender *trumps* grammatical gender. Even though most nouns that end in **x** are feminine, **rex** and **dux** are masculine because of natural gender.

♦ English words that show their 3rd declension origin by retaining the Latin plural ending **-es** are:

synopsis, synopses	*crisis, crises*	*index, indices*
appendix, appendices	*matrix, matrices*	*axis, axes*

> **Pax Romana** was the era of peace and prosperity that began with the principate of Caesar Augustus and continued for the next two hundred years. The British Empire was sometimes referred to as the *Pax Britannia* and the present world order is often called the *Pax Americana.*

Roman Empire

59

Caput Mundi   *Head of the World*

Third Declension   Neuter
stem: **nómin-**

Case	Singular	Ending	Plural	Ending
nom.	nomen	-	nómin**a**	-**a**
gen.	nómin**is**	-**is**	nómin**um**	-**um**
dat.	nómin**i**	-**i**	nómin**ibus**	-**ibus**
acc.	nomen	-	nómin**a**	-**a**
abl.	nómin**e**	-**e**	nómin**ibus**	-**ibus**

♦ **Nomen** is the model noun chosen to illustrate 3rd declension neuter nouns.

♦ There is no characteristic nominative singular ending for 3rd declension neuter nouns. The chart has a dash to show that the nominative singular form is variable.

♦ All nouns whose genitive singular ends in **is** belong to the 3rd declension.

♦ To find the stem, drop the genitive singular ending, **is**.

Vocabulary

caput cápitis	*n.*	head	*capital*
cor cordis	*n.*	heart	*cordial*
flumen flúminis	*n.*	river	*fluid*
lumen lúminis	*n.*	lamp	*luminous*
nomen nóminis	*n.*	name	*nominate*

♦ There are neuter nouns in the 2nd, 3rd, and 4th declensions. All neuter nouns obey the neuter rule:

the nominative and accusative case forms are identical

the nominative and accusative plural case ending is -a

♦ English words that show their 3rd declension neuter origin by retaining the Latin plural ending **-a** are:

corpus, corpora   *genus, genera*   *viscus, viscera*

> **Caput Mundi.** According to legend, workmen discovered a perfectly preserved human head while digging for the foundation of the Temple of Jupiter on the Saturnian Hill. When asked the meaning of this strange omen, the augurs responded that it meant Rome would become the head city of the world. The Saturnian Hill was renamed the Capitoline Hill from which we derive our word Capitol.

Oral Drill - Nominative Case

1.	cápita	1.	heart
2.	flumen	2.	lamps
3.	corda	3.	rivers
4.	pes	4.	names
5.	lúmina	5.	feet
6.	cor	6.	lamp
7.	duces	7.	river
8.	lumen	8.	heads
9.	flúmina	9.	leader
10.	caput	10.	head

Rex Regum   *King of Kings*

Third Declension Review

Case	Masculine/Feminine		Neuter	
	S.	Pl.	S.	Pl.
nom.	pater	patr**es**	nomen	nómin**a**
gen.	patr**is**	patr**um**	nómin**is**	nómin**um**
dat.	patr**i**	pátr**ibus**	nómin**i**	nomín**ibus**
acc.	patr**em**	patr**es**	nomen	nómin**a**
abl.	patr**e**	pátr**ibus**	nómin**e**	nomín**ibus**

♦ Contrast and compare the masculine, feminine, and neuter nouns of the 3rd declension. How are they alike and how are they different?

♦ All nouns whose genitive singular ends in **is** belong to the 3rd declension.

♦ To find the stem, drop the genitive singular ending, **is**.

Vocabulary Review

canis canis *m. or f.*	dog		**miles mílitis** *m.*	soldier
caput cápitis *n.*	head		**mos moris** *m.*	custom
cor cordis *n.*	heart		**nomen nóminis** *n.*	name
crux crucis *f.*	cross		**panis panis** *m.*	bread
dux ducis *m.*	leader		**pater patris** *m.*	father
flumen flúminis *n.*	river		**pax pacis** *f.*	peace
frater fratris *m.*	brother		**pes pedis** *m.*	foot
lex legis *f.*	law		**rex regis** *m.*	king
lumen lúminis *n.*	lamp		**sol solis** *m.*	sun
lux lucis *f.*	light		**soror sororis** *f.*	sister
mater matris *f.*	mother		**vox vocis** *f.*	voice

♦ The direct object of a verb is in the accusative case.
Regina laudat.   The queen praises. (no direct object)
Reginam laudat.   He (she) praises the queen. (queen is the direct object)

In the second sentence the subject must be in the verb because **reginam,** in the accusative case, cannot be a subject. See *Sentence Pattern #2* on page 97.

♦ Word order determines the subject and direct object in English, but not in Latin, where words can be in any order and still mean the same thing. The three sentences below all mean *Mary praises the queen.*

DO   SN   V-t   V-t   DO   SN   SN   DO   V-t
Reginam Maria laudat.   **Laudat reginam Maria.**   **Maria reginam laudat.**

♦ A common word order in Latin is: **subject   direct object   verb.**

Rex Regum. Christ is known as the *King of Kings.*

Oral Drill - Nominative case

1. **mílites**	1. fathers
2. **cápita**	2. heads
3. **nómina**	3. kings
4. **duces**	4. lamp
5. **flúmina**	5. soldier
6. **reges**	6. soldiers
7. **patres**	7. names
8. **soror**	8. customs
9. **leges**	9. voices
10. **canis**	10. sisters

Senatus Populúsque Romanus (S.P.Q.R.)
The Senate and People of Rome

Fourth Declension
stem **port-**

Case	Singular	Ending	Plural	Ending
nom.	port**us**	-us	port**ūs**	-ūs
gen.	port**ūs**	-ūs	pórt**uum**	-uum
dat.	pórt**ui**	-ui	pórt**ibus**	-ibus
acc.	port**um**	-um	port**ūs**	-ūs
abl.	port**u**	-u	pórt**ibus**	-ibus

♦ **Portus** is the model noun chosen to illustrate the *4th Declension*.

♦ All nouns whose genitive singular end in **-ūs** belong to the 4th declension.

♦ To find the stem, drop the genitive singular ending, **-ūs**.

♦ The genitive singular, nominative and accusative plural will be marked with macrons in this text to distinguish them from the nominative singular ending.

Vocabulary

adventus -ūs	*m.*	arrival	*advent*
domus -ūs	*f.*	house, home	*domestic*
exércitus -ūs	*m.*	army	*exercise*
fructus -ūs	*m.*	fruit	*fruit*
lacus -ūs	*m.*	lake	
manus -ūs	*f.*	hand	*manual, manufacture*
metus -ūs	*m.*	fear	
portus -ūs	*m.*	harbor	*port*
senatus -ūs	*m.*	senate	*senate*
spíritus -ūs	*m.*	spirit	*spirit*

◆ The gender rule for the 4th declension is **4D M**. Most 4th declension nouns are masculine. A few are feminine but both genders have the same endings. There are a few neuter nouns that have slightly different case endings. The 4th declension is a small declension with relatively few nouns.

◆ The 2nd, 3rd, and 4th declensions have nouns that end in **-us** in the nominative singular: You have had **-us** nouns in the 2nd and 4th declensions.

2nd declension	servus, servi
4th declension	portus, portūs

> **Senatus Populúsque Romanus. S.P.Q.R.** is the symbol of the Roman Republic written on all official government documents and monuments. It is similar to the *Office of the President* in America or *O.H.M.S., On Her Majesty's Service,* in England.

Oral Drill - Nominative Case

1.	portus	1.	hand
2.	manūs	2.	years
3.	annus	3.	houses
4.	fructus	4.	arrival
5.	spíritus	5.	harbors
6.	senatus	6.	fruit
7.	servus	7.	lakes
8.	lacūs	8.	spirits
9.	Christus	9.	fear
10.	exércitus	10.	slaves

Carpe diem. *Seize the day.*

Fifth Declension

stem **r-**

Case	Singular	Ending	Plural	Ending
nom.	r es	-es	r es	-es
gen.	r ei	-ei	r erum	-erum
dat.	r ei	-ei	r ebus	-ebus
acc.	r em	-em	r es	-es
abl.	r e	-e	r ebus	-ebus

♦ **Res** is the model noun chosen to illustrate the *5th Declension.*

♦ All nouns whose genitive singular end in **ei** belong to the 5th declension.

♦ To find the stem drop the genitive singular ending, **ei.**

Vocabulary

dies diei	*m.*	day	*diary*
fácies faciei	*f.*	face	*facial*
fides fidei	*f*	faith, trust	*fidelity*
res rei	*f.*	thing, matter, affair, business	*real*
spes spei	*f.*	hope	*despair*

♦ The gender rule for the 5th declension is **5D F.** Most 5th declension nouns are feminine. The 5th declension is small and has few nouns. A few are masculine, and none are neuter.

♦ Because the stem of a 5th declension noun can end in the letter **i**, a genitive singular form can have three consecutive vowels all of which are pronounced - **faciei.**

> **Carpe diem.** From one of Horace's *Odes*, **carpe diem** can be interpreted to mean, "make the most of today; take hold of the day and use it well, for tomorrow is not promised to you." Today is all you have.

Oral Drill - Nominative Case

1.	**fácies**	1.	days
2.	**dies**	2.	things
3.	**fides**	3.	face
4.	**miles**	4.	faces
5.	**milites**	5.	arrival
6.	**reges**	6.	trust
7.	**res**	7.	thing
8.	**flumina**	8.	hope
9.	**corda**	9.	faith
10.	**spes**	10.	home

UNIT IV REVIEW

Third, Fourth, Fifth Declensions

Case	3rd Declension M/F		3rd Declension Neuter	
	S.	Pl.	S.	Pl.
nom.	pater	patr**es**	nomen	nómin**a**
gen.	patr**is**	patr**um**	nómin**is**	nómin**um**
dat.	patr**i**	patr**ibus**	nómin**i**	nomín**ibus**
acc.	patr**em**	patr**es**	nomen	nómin**a**
abl.	patr**e**	patr**ibus**	nómin**e**	nomín**ibus**

Case	4th Declension		5th Declension	
	S.	Pl.	S.	Pl.
nom.	port**us**	port**ūs**	r**es**	r**es**
gen.	port**ūs**	pórt**uum**	r**ei**	r**erum**
dat.	pórt**ui**	pórt**ibus**	r**ei**	r**ebus**
acc.	port**um**	port**ūs**	r**em**	r**es**
abl.	port**u**	pórt**ibus**	r**e**	r**ebus**

♦ 1st and 2nd declension adjectives can modify nouns of the 1st-5th declensions. In each example below, the adjective agrees with its noun in gender, number and case, but not declension.

	Masc.	*Fem.*	*Neuter*
Nominative S.	**pater bonus**	**mater bona**	**nomen bonum**
	good father	*good mother*	*good name*
Accusative S.	**magnum exercitum**	**magnam fidem**	**magnum bellum**
	great army	*great faith*	*great war*

♦ If the genitive singular is -**is** the noun is 3rd declension. If the genitive singular is -**ūs**, the noun is 4th declension. If the genitive singular is -**ei**, the noun is 5th declension.

♦ The direct object of a verb is in the accusative case.

Vocabulary Review

adventus -ūs m.	*arrival*	**mater matris f.**	*mother*
canis canis m., f.	*dog*	**metus -ūs m.**	*fear*
caput cápitis n.	*head*	**miles mílitis m.**	*soldier*
cor cordis n.	*heart*	**mos moris m.**	*custom*
crux crucis f.	*cross*	**nomen nóminis n.**	*name*
dies -ei m.	*day*	**panis panis m.**	*bread*
domus -ūs f.	*house, home*	**pater patris m.**	*father*
dux ducis m.	*leader*	**pax pacis f.**	*peace*
exércitus -ūs m.	*army*	**pes pedis m.**	*foot*
fácies -ei f.	*face*	**portus -ūs m.**	*harbor*
fides -ei f.	*faith, trust*	**res -ei f.**	*thing, matter, affair, business*
flumen flúminis n.	*river*	**rex regis m.**	*king*
frater fratris m.	*brother*	**senatus -ūs m.**	*senate*
fructus -ūs m.	*fruit*	**sol solis m.**	*sun*
lacus -ūs m.	*lake*	**soror sororis f.**	*sister*
lex legis f.	*law*	**spes -ei f.**	*hope*
lumen lúminis n.	*lamp*	**spíritus -ūs m.**	*spirit*
lux lucis f.	*light*	**vox vocis f.**	*voice*
manus -ūs f.	*hand*		

Latin Sayings

alma mater
Pax Romana
Rex Regum

Caput Mundi
Senatus Populúsque Romanus (S.P.Q.R.)
Carpe diem.

UNITS III AND IV REVIEW

The Five Declensions

Case	1st Declension S.	1st Declension Pl.	2nd Declension Masc. S.	2nd Declension Masc. Pl.	2nd Declension Neuter S.	2nd Declension Neuter Pl.
nom.	mens**a**	mens**ae**	serv**us**	serv**i**	bell**um**	bell**a**
gen.	mens**ae**	mens**arum**	serv**i**	serv**orum**	bell**i**	bell**orum**
dat.	mens**ae**	mens**is**	serv**o**	serv**is**	bell**o**	bell**is**
acc.	mens**am**	mens**as**	serv**um**	serv**os**	bell**um**	bell**a**
abl.	mens**ā**	mens**is**	serv**o**	serv**is**	bell**o**	bell**is**

Case	3rd Declension M/F S.	3rd Declension M/F Pl.	3rd Declension Neuter S.	3rd Declension Neuter Pl.
nom.	pater	patr**es**	nomen	nómin**a**
gen.	patr**is**	patr**um**	nómin**is**	nómin**um**
dat.	patr**i**	pátr**ibus**	nómin**i**	nomín**ibus**
acc.	patr**em**	patr**es**	nomen	nómin**a**
abl.	patr**e**	pátr**ibus**	nómin**e**	nomín**ibus**

Case	4th Declension S.	4th Declension Pl.	5th Declension S.	5th Declension Pl.
nom.	port**us**	port**ūs**	r**es**	r**es**
gen.	port**ūs**	pórt**uum**	r**ei**	r**erum**
dat.	pórt**ui**	pórt**ibus**	r**ei**	r**ebus**
acc.	port**um**	port**ūs**	r**em**	r**es**
abl.	port**u**	pórt**ibus**	r**e**	r**ebus**

Vocabulary Review: Units III and IV

adventus -ūs m. *arrival*

aeternus -a -um *eternal, everlasting*

agnus -i m. *lamb*

agrícola -ae m. *farmer*

altus -a -um *high, deep*

amicus -i m. *friend*

annus -i m. *year*

bellum -i n. *war*

bonus -a -um *good*

caelum -i n. *sky, heaven*

canis canis m. f. *dog*

caput cápitis n. *head*

Christus -i m. *Christ*

cor cordis n. *heart*

crux crucis f. *cross*

débitum -i n. *debt, sin*

deus -i m. *god*

dies -ei m. *day*

dóminus -i m. *lord, master*

domus -ūs f. *house, home*

donum -i n. *gift*

dux ducis m. *leader*

equus -i m. *horse*

exércitus -ūs m. *army*

fácies -ei f. *face*

fides -ei f. *faith, trust*

fílius -i m. *son*

flumen flúminis n. *river*

forum -i n. *forum, marketplace*

frater fratris m. *brother*

fructus -ūs m. *fruit*

Itália -ae f. *Italy*

lacus -ūs m. *lake*

latus -a -um *wide, broad*

lex legis f. *law*

lumen lúminis n. *lamp*

lux lucis f. *light*

magnus -a -um *great, large*

malus -a -um *bad*

manus -ūs f. *hand*

Maria -ae f. *Mary*

mater matris f. *mother*

mensa -ae f. *table*

metus -ūs m. *fear*

miles mílitis m. *soldier*

mos moris m. *custom*

multus -a -um *much, many*

mundus -i m. *world, mankind*

nauta -ae m. *sailor*

nomen nóminis n. *name*

novus -a -um *new*

óppidum -i n. *town*

panis panis m. *bread*

parvus -a -um *small*

pater patris m. *father*

pax pacis f. *peace*

pes pedis m. *foot*

poeta -ae m. *poet*

portus -ūs m. *harbor*

puella -ae f. *girl*

regina -ae f. *queen*

regnum -i n. *kingdom*

res -ei f. *thing, matter, affair, business*

rex regis m. *king*

Roma -ae f. *Rome*

sanctus -a -um *sacred, holy*

saxum -i n. *rock*

senatus -ūs m. *senate*

servus -i m. *slave, servant*

sol solis m. *sun*

soror sororis f. *sister*

spes -ei f. *hope*

spíritus -ūs m. *spirit*

templum -i n. *temple*

terra -ae f. *earth, land*

verbum -i n. *word*

vox vocis f. *voice*

UNIT V INTRODUCTION

♦ The 1st and 2nd Conjugations are very similar.

♦ The Present System consists of the three tenses built on the **present stem**: the present tense, the imperfect tense, and the future tense.

♦ The present stem is found by dropping the **re** from the 2nd Conjugation infinitive ending, **ēre**. The stem vowel of the 2nd conjugation is **ē.**

♦ The Perfect System consists of the three tenses built on the perfect stem: the perfect tense, the pluperfect tense, and future perfect tense. The perfect stem is found by dropping the **i** from the 3rd principal part.

♦ The tense endings for the 1st and 2nd conjugations are identical.

♦ The 3rd and 4th conjugations are similar and will be studied in Second Form.

♦ Verbs are classified into conjugations by the infinitive.

Conjugation	Infinitive ending
1st	**-are**
2nd	**-ēre**
3rd	**-ere**
4th	**-ire**

UNIT V

VERBS
2ND CONJUGATION
PRESENT AND PERFECT SYSTEMS

The Pantheon

Marcus Agrippa built and dedicated the original Pantheon after the Battle of Actium (31 B.C.) as a temple to all the gods of Rome. The original building was destroyed by fire and was rebuilt by the emperor Hadrian in the 2nd century. It is the best preserved of Rome's ancient buildings and survives largely because it has never been out of use—it was converted to a church in the 7th century. Today it faces one of the most popular piazzas in Rome.

Vídeo et táceo. *I see and am silent.*

Second Conjugation - Present Tense

Person	Singular		Plural	
1st	móne**o**	I warn	mone**mus**	we warn
2nd	mone**s**	you warn	mone**tis**	you warn
3rd	mone**t**	he, she, it warns	mone**nt**	they warn

♦ **Móneo** is the model verb chosen to illustrate the *2nd Conjugation*. All verbs in the vocabulary list are conjugated like **móneo**.

♦ The infinitive of **móneo** is **monēre**. The infinitive ending is **ēre**. All verbs whose infinitive ends in **ēre** are 2nd conjugation verbs. The **ē** of the infinitive is marked with a macron to distinguish it from the 3rd conjugation infinitive (not covered in this text).

♦ To find the present stem of a 2nd conjugation verb, drop the **re** from the infinitive.

monēre **monē/re** **stem = monē**

Vocabulary

débeo -ēre	to owe, ought	*debt*
dóceo -ēre*	to teach	*docile*
gáudeo -ēre*	to rejoice	*gaudy*
hábeo -ēre	to have	*habit*
móneo -ēre	to warn	*monitor*
móveo -ēre*	to move	*movable*
sédeo -ēre*	to sit	*sedate*
táceo -ēre	to be silent	*taciturn*
téneo -ēre*	to hold	*tentacle*
vídeo -ēre*	to see	*video*

* Irregular principal parts; see Lessons 31-32

♦ The stem vowel of the 2nd conjugation is **ē.** The present tense is formed by adding the personal endings to the present stem **monē.** Notice that the 1st person singular form **moneo** retains the stem vowel **e,** rather than losing it like the 1st conjugation **amo.**

♦ The complementary infinitive is often used with **débeo.** The infinitive may precede or follow the main verb. See *Sentence Pattern #2*, page 97.

> **Ambulare débeo.**   I ought to walk.
>
> **Debes sedēre.**   You ought to sit.

Vídeo et táceo. The classic statement of discretion, this saying is attributed to Queen Elizabeth I, daughter of Henry VIII. A monarch must be discreet, reasonably merciful, and not judge everything that she sees. And yet, there is an undertone of irony and even threat in this statement: "Mind you, I do see everything."

Oral Drill

1. **debet** he owes
2. **sédeo** to sit
3. **monetis** y'all warn
4. **doces** you teach
5. **tenent** they hold
6. **videt** he sees
7. **gaudemus** we rejoice
8. **táceo** be silent
9. **movent** they move
10. **habet** he has

1. we are silent tacemus
2. they owe debet
3. I move moneo
4. she sees videt
5. you warn mones
6. he has habet
7. we hold tenemus
8. you ought debes
9. I rejoice gaudeo
10. they are sitting sedent

75

Cave canem. *Beware the dog.*

Second Conjugation - Imperfect and Future Tenses

Imperfect			
mone**bam**	I was warning	mone**bamus**	we were warning
mone**bas**	you were warning	mone**batis**	you were warning
mone**bat**	he, she, it was warning	mone**bant**	they were warning
Future			
mone**bo**	I will warn	moné**bimus**	we will warn
mone**bis**	you will warn	moné**bitis**	you will warn
mone**bit**	he, she, it will warn	mone**bunt**	they will warn

◆ The imperfect and future tense endings are identical to those of the 1st conjugation.

Vocabulary

appáreo -ēre	to appear	*appearance*
árdeo -ēre*	to burn, be on fire	*arson*
cáveo -ēre*	to beware of, guard against	*caution*
júbeo -ēre*	to order, command	
máneo -ēre*	to remain, stay	*mansion*
prohíbeo -ēre	to prevent	*prohibit*
respóndeo -ēre*	to respond, answer	*response*
térreo -ēre	to frighten	*terrify*
tímeo -ēre*	to fear, be afraid of	*timid*
váleo -ēre*	to be strong, be well	*valor*

* Irregular principal parts; see Lessons 31-32

♦ **Tímeo** is often used with the complementary infinitive. See *Sentence Pattern #2*, page 97.

Pugnare tímeo.
to fight   I am afraid
I am afraid to fight.

Timemus natare.
we fear   to swim
We fear to swim.

Cave canem was as familiar a phrase to the ancient Romans as it is to us. Many Roman houses had the image of a ferocious dog portrayed in mosaic at the front entrance.

Oral Drill

1. **debebat**	1. I will warn
2. **valebo**	2. you were frightening
3. **habebunt**	3. they will respond
4. **prohibemus**	4. we are being silent
5. **terres**	5. you will appear
6. **apparebant**	6. it was preventing
7. **tacent**	7. I was being silent
8. **monébitis**	8. they ought
9. **debebit**	9. we appear
10. **habebant**	10. she has

Docēre, delectare, movēre
To teach, to delight, to move

Second Conjugation   Principal Parts

1st	2nd	3rd	4th
món**eo**	mon**ēre**	món**ui**	món**itus**
I warn	to warn	I warned	warned
eo	**ēre**	**ui**	**itus**

♦ The regular principal parts with regular endings for the 2nd conjugation are given above. Notice the similarities and differences with the 1st conjugation principal parts.

♦ In a vocabulary list or dictionary entry, a verb that is followed by **(2)** or **ēre**, has regular principal parts. If the principal parts are irregular, they will be written out in full.

♦ To write the principal parts of regular 2nd conjugation verbs, drop the **eo** from the first principal part and add the regular endings **ēre, ui, itus.**

Second Conjugation - Present System

Present Tense	
móne**o**	mone**mus**
mone**s**	mone**tis**
mone**t**	mone**nt**
Imperfect Tense	
mone**bam**	mone**bamus**
mone**bas**	mone**batis**
mone**bat**	mone**bant**
Future Tense	
mone**bo**	moné**bimus**
mone**bis**	moné**bitis**
mone**bit**	mone**bunt**

♦ Say each verb with its regular principal parts.

móneo (2)	*to warn*
appáreo (2)	*to appear*
débeo (2)	*to owe, ought*
hábeo (2)	*to have*
prohíbeo (2)	*to prevent*
térreo (2)	*to frighten*
táceo (2)	*to be silent*

♦ These verbs have irregular principal parts. Each one must be learned individually. Say each one aloud many times, until you know them all perfectly.

1st	2nd	3rd	4th
tímeo	**timēre**	**tímui**	--
váleo	**valēre**	**válui**	--
dóceo	**docēre**	**dócui**	doctus
téneo	**tenēre**	**ténui**	tentus
árdeo	**ardēre**	arsi	arsus
júbeo	**jubēre**	jussi	jussus
máneo	**manēre**	mansi	mansus

Docēre, delectare, movēre is a paraphrase of one of Quintilian's principles of oratory. The speaker should not only instruct his audience, but move them and delight them as well. The triplet was used by St. Augustine and by many rhetoricians of the Renaissance. It is the motto of *Highlands Latin School* in Louisville, Kentucky.

Veni, vidi, vici. *I came, I saw, I conquered.*

Second Conjugation - Perfect System

Perfect			
món**ui**	I have warned	monú**imus**	we have warned
monu**isti**	you have warned	monu**istis**	you have warned
mónu**it**	hsi has warned	monu**erunt**	they have warned
Pluperfect			
monú**eram**	I had warned	monu**eramus**	we had warned
monú**eras**	you had warned	monu**eratis**	you had warned
monú**erat**	hsi had warned	monú**erant**	they had warned
Future Perfect			
monú**ero**	I will have warned	monu**érimus**	we will have warned
monú**eris**	you will have warned	monú**éritis**	you will have warned
monú**erit**	hsi will have warned	monú**erint**	they will have warned

♦ These verbs have irregular principal parts. Each one must be learned individually. Say each one aloud until you know them all perfectly.

1st	2nd	3rd	4th
gáudeo*	**gaudēre**	--	--
cáveo	**cavēre**	**cavi**	**cautus**
sédeo	**sedēre**	**sedi**	**sessus**
vídeo	**vidēre**	**vidi**	**visus**
respóndeo	**respondēre**	**respondi**	**responsus**
móveo	**movēre**	**movi**	**motus**

***Gáudeo** is irregular in the perfect system.

- The Perfect System consists of three tenses: perfect, pluperfect, and future perfect.

- The Perfect System is built on the perfect stem.

- To find the perfect stem drop the personal ending **i** from the 3rd principal part.

móneo monēre mónui mónitus

monu/i = monu

- The tense endings for the perfect system of the 2nd conjugation are identical to those of the 1st conjugation, as are the meanings.

Julius Caesar

Veni, vidi, vici. In 47 B.C., Julius Caesar defeated the king of Pontus in one hour. He was so proud of his extraordinary speed that he sent the famous message to the Senate in Rome: **veni vidi vici.** A successful general was allowed to have a victory parade, called a *triumph.* There was a grand procession along the Via Sacra in the Forum in which the general showed off his prisoners, the spoils of victory, and displays relating to the events of the campaign. Caesar's Pontic triumph was unusual in that the central place was given to a placard bearing the simple inscription

Veni Vidi Vici.

UNIT V REVIEW

Second Conjugation   Indicative Active

present stem: **monē-**

Present	
móne**o**	mone**mus**
mone**s**	mone**tis**
mone**t**	mone**nt**

Imperfect	
mone**bam**	mone**bamus**
mone**bas**	mone**batis**
mone**bat**	mone**bant**

Future	
mone**bo**	moné**bimus**
mone**bis**	moné**bitis**
mone**bit**	mone**bunt**

perfect stem: **monu-**

Perfect	
mónu**i**	monú**imus**
monu**isti**	monu**istis**
mónu**it**	monu**erunt**

Pluperfect	
monú**eram**	monu**eramus**
monú**eras**	monu**eratis**
monú**erat**	monú**erant**

Future Perfect	
monú**ero**	monu**érimus**
monú**eris**	monu**ēritis**
monú**erit**	monú**erint**

Vocabulary Review

móneo (2)	*to warn*
appáreo (2)	*to appear*
débeo (2)	*to owe, ought*
hábeo (2)	*to have*
prohíbeo (2)	*to prevent*
térreo (2)	*to frighten*
táceo (2)	*to be silent*

1st	2nd	3rd	4th	Meaning
tímeo	**timēre**	**tímui**	—	*to fear, be afraid of*
váleo	**valēre**	**válui**	—	*to be strong, be well*
dóceo	**docēre**	**dócui**	**doctus**	*to teach*
téneo	**tenēre**	**ténui**	**tentus**	*to hold*
árdeo	**ardēre**	**arsi**	**arsus**	*to burn, be on fire*
júbeo	**jubēre**	**jussi**	**jussus**	*to order, command*
máneo	**manēre**	**mansi**	**mansus**	*to remain, stay*
gáudeo	**gaudēre**	—	—	*to rejoice*
cáveo	**cavēre**	**cavi**	**cautus**	*to beware of, guard against*
sédeo	**sedēre**	**sedi**	**sessus**	*to sit*
vídeo	**vidēre**	**vidi**	**visus**	*to see*
respóndeo	**respondēre**	**respondi**	**responsus**	*to respond, answer*
móveo	**movēre**	**movi**	**motus**	*to move*

Latin Sayings

Vídeo et táceo.
Cave canem.

Docēre, delectare, movēre
Veni, vidi, vici.

Verb Review - Units I, II, and V

Tense	Number	1st Conjugation	2nd Conjugation	Sum
Present	*sing.*	amo	móneo	sum
		amas	mones	es
		amat	monet	est
	pl.	amamus	monemus	sumus
		amatis	monetis	estis
		amant	monent	sunt
Imperfect	*sing.*	amabam	monebam	eram
		amabas	monebas	eras
		amabat	monebat	erat
	pl.	amabamus	monebamus	eramus
		amabatis	monebatis	eratis
		amabant	monebant	erant
Future	*sing.*	amabo	monebo	ero
		amabis	monebis	eris
		amabit	monebit	erit
	pl.	amábimus	monébimus	érimus
		amábitis	monébitis	éritis
		amabunt	monebunt	erunt
Perfect	*sing.*	amavi	mónui	fui
		amavisti	monuisti	fuisti
		amavit	mónuit	fuit
	pl.	amávimus	monúimus	fúimus
		amavistis	monuistis	fuistis
		amaverunt	monuerunt	fuerunt
Pluperfect	*sing.*	amáveram	monúeram	fúeram
		amáveras	monúeras	fúeras
		amáverat	monúerat	fúerat
	pl.	amaveramus	monueramus	fueramus
		amaveratis	monueratis	fueratis
		amáverant	monúerant	fúerant
Future perfect	*sing.*	amávero	monúero	fúero
		amáveris	monúeris	fúeris
		amáverit	monúerit	fúerit
	pl.	amavérimus	monuérimus	fuérimus
		amavéritis	monuéritis	fuéritis
		amáverint	monúerint	fúerint

FIRST - SECOND CONJUGATION VERBS

accuso (1)	to accuse	**narro (1)**	to tell
adoro (1)	to adore	**nato (1)**	to swim
ámbulo (1)	to walk	**návigo (1)**	to sail
amo (1)	to love, like	**nego (1)**	to deny
appáreo (2)	to appear	**núntio (1)**	to report
appello (1)	to address	**óccupo (1)**	to seize
árdeo -ēre arsi arsus	to burn, be on fire	**oppugno (1)**	to attack
aro (1)	to plow	**opto (1)**	to desire, wish
cáveo -ēre cavi cautus	to beware of, guard against	**oro (1)**	to speak, pray
celo (1)	to hide	**paro (1)**	to prepare
clamo (1)	to shout	**perturbo (1)**	to disturb
creo (1)	to create	**porto (1)**	to carry
culpo (1)	to blame	**prohíbeo (2)**	to prevent
débeo (2)	to owe, ought	**pugno (1)**	to fight
delecto (1)	to delight, please	**puto (1)**	to think
demonstro (1)	to show, point out	**respóndeo -ēre respondi responsus**	to respond, answer
do -are dedi datus	to give		
dóceo -ēre dócui doctus	to teach	**rogo (1)**	to ask
dúbito (1)	to doubt	**saluto (1)**	to greet
erro (1)	to err, wander	**sédeo -ēre sedi sessus**	to sit
exploro (1)	to explore	**servo (1)**	to guard, keep
exspecto (1)	to wait for, expect	**specto (1)**	to look at
gáudeo -ēre -- --	to rejoice	**spero (1)**	to hope
hábeo (2)	to have	**sto -are steti status**	to stand
hábito (1)	to live in, dwell	**súpero (1)**	to overcome
júbeo -ēre jussi jussus	to order, command	**táceo (2)**	to be silent
júdico (1)	to judge, consider	**tempto (1)**	to tempt
juvo -are juvi jutus	to help	**téneo -ēre ténui tentus**	to hold
laboro (1)	to work	**térreo (2)**	to frighten
laudo (1)	to praise	**tímeo -ēre timui --**	to fear, be afraid of
lavo -are lavi lautus	to wash	**váleo -ēre válui --**	to be strong, be well
líbero (1)	to set free	**vídeo -ēre vidi visus**	to see
máneo -ēre mansi mansus	to remain, stay	**voco (1)**	to call
móneo (2)	to warn	**volo (1)**	to fly
móveo -ēre movi motus	to move	**vúlnero (1)**	to wound
muto (1)	to change		
		sum esse fui futurus	to be

APPENDICES

Everyday Latin

Salve (salvete)*	*Greetings, hello*
Vale (valete)	*Good bye*
Quid est nomen tibi?	*What is your name?*
Mihi nomen est...	*My name is...*
Quid agis?	*How are you?*
Valeo.	*I am well.*
Admirábilis	*Wonderful*
Grátias tibi ago.	*Thank you.*
Optatus venis	*You are most welcome.*
Ignosce mihi, quaeso	*Pardon (excuse) me, please.*
Sodes	*Please (would you mind, if you don't mind)*
Me paénitet	*I'm sorry.*
Te amo	*I love you.*
(Ego amo te)	*I love you. (Not as correct but a student favorite)*
Ita	*Yes.*

Classroom Latin

Salvete, amici Latinae.	*Greetings, friends of Latin.*
Salvete, discípuli.	*Hello, students.*
Salve, magister/magistra. *(m/f)*	*Greetings (hello), teacher.*
Salve, discípule.	*Hello, student.*
Vale, magister/magistra.*(m/f)*	*Good bye, teacher.*
Valete, discípuli.	*Good bye, students.*
Sede (sedete)	*Sit down.*
Surge (súrgite)	*Stand up.*
Adsum	*Present*
Aperi (aperite)	*Open*
Claude (cláudite)	*Close*
jánuam	*door*
fenestram, fenestras	*window, windows*
librum, libros	*book, books*

*The words in parentheses are plural commands or greetings.

Audi (audite) diligenter.	*Listen carefully*
Impossíbile est.	*That is impossible.*
Est-ne confusus?	*Are you puzzled?*
Explica, quaeso	*Please explain.*
Non intéllego	*I don't understand.*
Adjuva (adjuvate) me	*Help me.*
Fallit	*It is wrong.*
Falsus	*Wrong, incorrect*
Verum	*Correct*
Siléntium, quaeso	*Silence, please*
Tace (tacete)	*Be silent*
Ad páginam	*Turn to page*
Responde mihi	*Answer me*
Oremus.	*Let us pray.*
Bene actum	*Well done.*
Óptime!	*Excellent!*
Péssime!	*Very bad!*
Scribe (scribite) haec verba	*Write these words*
Fiat	*All right (let it be done).*
De hoc satis	*Enough of this!*
Collige fólia	*Collect the papers.*
Quid dixit, dixisti	*What did he say? you say?*

Signum Crucis

In nómine Patris et Fílii et Spíritus Sancti.

Pater Noster

Pater Noster, Qui es in Caelis. Sanctificetur Nomen Tuum. Advéniat Regnum Tuum, fiat voluntas Tua, sicut in Caelo et in terra. Panem nostrum cotidianum da nobis hódie. Et dimitte nobis débita nostra, sicut et nos dimíttimus debitóribus nostris, et ne nos inducas in tentationem, sed líbera nos a malo.

Table Blessing

Benedíc Dómine nos et haec tua dona quae de tua largitate sumus sumpturi.

Per Christum Dóminum Nostrum. Amen.

Doxology (Glória Patri)

Glória Patri et Fílio et Spirítui Sancto. Sicut erat in princípio et nunc et semper et in saécula saeculorum. Amen

Sanctus and Benedictus

Sanctus, Sanctus, Sanctus, Dóminus Deus Sábaoth. Pleni sunt Caeli et terra glória Tua. Hosanna in Excelsis. Benedictus qui venit in nómine Dómini. Hosanna in Excelsis.

Agnus Dei

Agnus Dei, qui tollis peccata mundi, miserere nobis.
Agnus Dei, qui tollis peccata mundi, miserere nobis.
Agnus Dei, qui tollis peccata mundi, dona nobis pacem.

Ave Maria

Ave Maria, grátia plena, Dóminus tecum. Benedicta tu in muliéribus, et benedictus fructus ventris tui, Jesus.

Sancta Maria, Mater Dei, ora pro nobis peccatóribus. Nunc et in hora mortis nostrae. Amen.

Sign of the Cross

In the name of the Father, the Son and the Holy Ghost.

Our Father

Our Father, who art in Heaven. Hallowed be thy name. Thy Kingdom come, thy will be done, on earth as it is in Heaven. Give us this day our daily bread and forgive us our trespasses as we forgive those who trespass against us, and lead us not into temptation but deliver us from evil.

Table Blessing

Bless us O Lord and these thy gifts which we are about to receive from thy bounty. Through Christ Our Lord, Amen.

Doxology

Glory be to the Father, and to the Son, and to the Holy Spirit. As it was in the beginning, is now and ever shall be, world without end. Amen.

Sanctus and Benedictus

Holy, Holy, Holy, Lord God of Hosts. Heaven and earth are full of Your glory. Hosanna in the highest. Blessed is he who comes in the name of the Lord. Hosanna in the highest.

Agnus Dei

Lamb of God, you take away the sins of the world, have mercy on us.
Lamb of God, you take away the sins of the world, have mercy on us.
Lamb of God, you take away the sins of the world, grant us peace.

Hail Mary

Hail Mary, full of grace, The Lord is with thee, Blessed art thou among women And blessed is the fruit of thy womb, Jesus

Holy Mary, Mother of God, Pray for us sinners, Now and at the hour of our death. Amen.

alma mater*	*nurturing mother*
Anno Dómini (A.D.)*	*In the year of our Lord*
ante bellum*	*before the war*
Caput Mundi	*Head of the World*
Carpe diem.	*Seize the day.*
Cave canem.	*Beware the dog.*
Civis Romanus sum.	*I am a Roman citizen.*
Docēre, delectare, movēre	*To teach, to delight, to move*
Errare est humanum.	*To err is human.*
Fortes fortuna juvat.	*Fortune aids the brave.*
In choro recitemus.	*Let us recite together.*
In umbra, ígitur, pugnábimus.	*Then we will fight in the shade.*
Mater Itáliae Roma*	*The mother of Italy, Rome*
nunc aut numquam*	*now or never*
Ora et labora.*	*Pray and work.*
Pax Romana*	*The Roman Peace*
Quattuor anni témpora	*The four seasons of the year*
Rex Regum	*King of Kings*
Roma Aeterna	*Eternal Rome*
semper fidelis*	*always faithful*
Senatus Populúsque Romanus (SPQR)*	*The Senate and People of Rome*
Stabat Mater	*The Mother was Standing*
Veni, vidi, vici.*	*I came, I saw, I conquered.*
Vídeo et táceo.	*I see and am silent.*

*Sayings also in *Latina Christiana*

A sentence is a complete thought and is made of two basic parts, the **subject** and the **predicate**.

subject   predicate

The subject is **what** or **who** the sentence is about.
The predicate tells what the subject **is** or **does**.

The *complete subject* contains the subject with all of its modifiers. The *simple subject* is usually just called the subject. The *complete predicate* contains the simple predicate and its modifiers. The simple predicate is called the *verb*. Modifiers in the subject and predicate do not change the basic structure of the sentence.

simple subject   simple predicate (main verb with helping verbs)

Shouting with joy, Mary   **was skipping through the garden yesterday.**
complete subject   complete predicate

One way to help students understand grammar is to label each word in a sentence. Here is a list of sentence parts and their abbreviations. Students can write these abbreviations above each word and then diagram each sentence. Here are the labels that will be used in this text.

Subject noun	SN
Subject pronoun	SP
Subject (personal ending - Latin verb)	SPE
Verb	V
Verb-transitive	V-t
Linking verb	LV
Article	A
Adjective	Adj
Adverb	Adv
Predicate adjective	PA
Predicate nominative	PrN
Direct object	DO
Complementary infinitive	CI

Action Verbs

Action verbs express action, either seen, such as *do, run, write* and *go,* or unseen such as *think, believe,* and *know.*

Action verbs can be *transitive* or *intransitive.* Most verbs are transitive because they express action that can be passed from the subject to another person or thing in the sentence, the direct object.

<pre>
       SN   V-t   DO
      Ben eats the sandwich.
</pre>

Eat is a transitive verb because the action is passed from the subject to the direct object, the *sandwich.*

Some verbs, by their nature, cannot take a direct object.

Ben is sleeping. Ben will arrive late.

Sleep and *arrive* are intransitive. The action cannot be passed on to another person or thing in the sentence. (*Late* is an adverb, not a direct object.)

State of Being Verbs

A state of being verb expresses existence or state of being. It does not express action, and therefore by definition is *intransitive.*

The most common state of being verb is the *to be* verb, whose forms in English are *am, is, are, was, were, be, being, been.*

The *to be* verb is usually a linking verb, linking the subject to a word in the predicate that names or describes the subject.

<pre>
     SN   LV   PrN   SN LV   PA
    Ben was a soldier.   Ben is strong.
</pre>

In these sentences, the noun that renames the subject is called the predicate nominative (PrN) and the adjective that describes the subject is called the predicate adjective (PA).

There are seven basic sentence patterns. Four will be presented in this text. Each of these sentence patterns will be labeled and diagrammed.

Diagramming

Diagramming gives students a picture of sentence structure, and is another effective technique to help students understand grammar. The diagram begins with a horizontal line that contains the backbone of the sentence—the subject and the verb. Crossing over this line is a vertical line that divides the sentence into its two parts, the simple subject on the left and the verb on the right. Adjectives and adverbs are written on slanted lines below the words they modify.

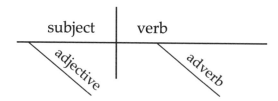

Complements are written on the horizontal line and separated from the verb by a line which <u>does not</u> cross over the base line. If the complement is a direct object, the vertical line is perpendicular to the base line.

subject	verb	direct object

If the complement is a predicate nominative or adjective, the vertical line is slanted to the left.

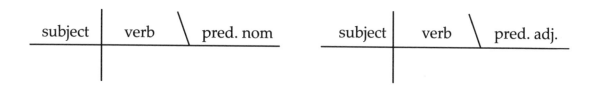

Sentence Pattern #1
Subject + Verb

If an action verb is intransitive, all that is needed for a sentence is the backbone—a subject and a verb. The subject can be a noun or a pronoun, and other modifiers, such as adverbs and adjectives, do not change the basic pattern.

The verb can be one word or it can be a verb phrase. A verb phrase contains a main verb plus all of its helping verbs. In this text we will underline the verb phrase when labeling sentences.

SN   V   Adv

Mary <u>is walking</u> today.

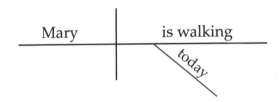

In Latin, the subject of a sentence can be the personal ending of the verb (SPE). Here is a model for diagramming and labeling this kind of sentence in both English and Latin.

V   SPE   SP   V

Ambul(o)   **I walk.**

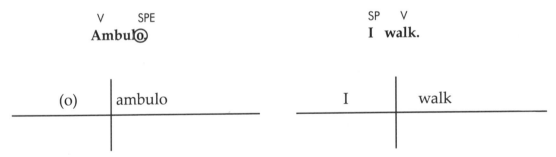

Sentence Patterns #2 through #4

Sentence Pattern #1 above is the only one of the seven basic sentence patterns that does <u>not</u> have **complements**. Most verbs need a completer to *complete* their meaning. If I say *Mary likes*, you do not feel like I have finished my thought. You want to know *what Mary likes*. All of the six remaining sentence patterns have complements. We will learn three complements in this text: the *direct object, predicate nominative*, and *predicate adjective*.

Sentence Pattern #2
Subject + Verb + Direct Object

The first type of complement is the direct object. Typical English word order is *subject-verb-direct object*. Typical Latin word order is *subject-direct object-verb*. Diagramming follows English word order.

The direct object can be a noun or pronoun …

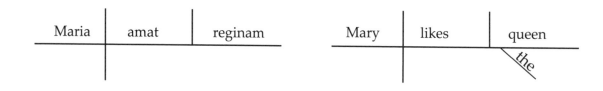

SN   DO   V-t
Maria reginam amat.

SN   V-t   DO
Mary likes the queen.

| Maria | amat | reginam |

| Mary | likes | queen / the |

or other more complex constructions, such as the *Complementary Infinitive (CI)*.

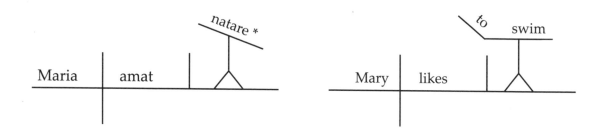

SN   CI   V-t
Maria natare amat.

SN   V-t   CI
Mary likes <u>to swim</u>.

* We are using a single slanted line here because "to swim" is one word in Latin.

Sentence Pattern #3
Subject + Verb + Predicate Adjective

Verbs that are completed by a predicate nominative or adjective are called *linking verbs.* They are *intransitive* because they are not completed by a direct object. If an adjective follows the linking verb and describes the subject, it is called a *predicate adjective* and is in the nominative case.

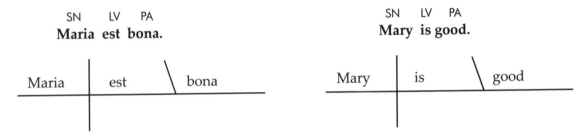

Sentence Pattern #4
Subject + Verb + Predicate Nominative

If a noun follows the linking verb and renames the subject, it is called a *predicate nominative* and is in the nominative case.

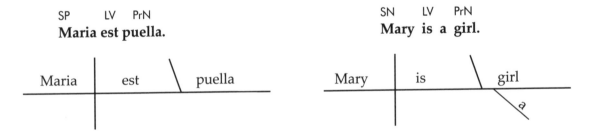

Again, modifiers do not change the basic sentence pattern.

SN   LV   Adj   PrN   Adv
Mary is a good girl today.

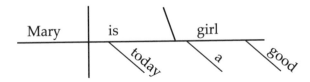

This chart provides a more detailed breakdown of specific Latin sentence patterns.

Sentence Type	Lesson Introduced	Symbols			Examples	Description
#1a	Lesson 2	SPE	V		**Ámbulat.** *She walks.*	Personal ending subject + action verb
#1b	Lesson 17	SN	V		**Maria ámbulat.** *Mary is walking. (Mary walks.)*	Noun subject + action verb
#2a	Lesson 7	SPE	V-t	CI	**Amat ámbulare.** *She loves to walk.*	Personal ending subject + action verb + complementary infinitive
#2b	Lesson 17	SN	V-t	CI	**Maria ámbulare amat.** *Mary loves to walk.*	Noun subject + action verb + complementary infinitive
#2c	Lesson 24	SPE	V-t	DO	**Reginam laudat.** *She praises the queen.*	Personal ending subject + action verb + direct object
#2d	Lesson 24	SN	V-t	DO	**Maria reginam laudat.** *Mary praises the queen.*	Noun subject + action verb + direct object
#3	Lesson 19	SN	LV	PA	**Maria est bona.** *Mary is good.*	Noun subject + linking verb + predicate adjective
#4	Lesson 19	SN	LV	PrN	**Maria est puella.** *Mary is a girl.*	Noun subject + linking verb + predicate nominative

Parts of Speech

Grammar is the study of how language works—how it enables humans to communicate thoughts. There are eight kinds of words, or *parts of speech*. Here is a quick way to remember them:

1. *What are the most important kinds of words?*	Nouns
2. *What words modify nouns?*	Adjectives
3. *What words take the place of nouns?*	Pronouns
4. *What are the second most important kinds of words?*	Verbs
5. *What words modify verbs?*	Adverbs
6. *What three parts of speech end with* **tion**?	Prepositions
	Conjunctions
	Interjections

Part of Speech	Definition	Examples	Latin Roots
noun	names a person, place, thing	*John, Rome, book*	**nomen**
verb	shows action or state of being	*see, think, eat*	**verbum**
adjective	modifies a noun or pronoun	*big, red, many*	**ad jácere**
adverb	modifies verb, adjective, or adverb	*quickly, now*	**ad verbum**
pronoun	takes place of noun	*I, you, who*	**pronomen**
preposition	shows relationship of a noun or pronoun to another word	*in, on, about, with*	**prae positio**
conjunction	joins words	*and, but, or*	**con júngere**
interjection	an exclamation that is not part of sentence	*Oh! Whew!*	**inter jácere**

(*The, a,* and *an* are called *articles* and are considered adjectives.)

Words used as more than one part of speech

An individual word can be more than one part of speech depending on how it is used in a sentence.

The **total** is sixty.	*noun*
It was a **total** disaster.	*adjective*
He will **total** the score.	*verb*

Parts of a Sentence

Words are used to communicate thoughts. A sentence is a complete thought, created first in the human mind. A sentence has two parts: a subject and a predicate. The subject is what the sentence is about, and the predicate tells what the subject *is* or *does*. Every sentence, no matter how long or complicated, can be divided into these two parts:

subject	who or what the sentence is about
predicate	what the subject *is* or *does*

Example:

The pretty girl gave me a wave and a wink in the garden. Wow!

Sentence Part	Definition	Example
simple subject	who or what the sentence is about	girl
complete subject	subject and its modifiers	The pretty girl
complete predicate	tells something about subject	gave me a wave and wink in the garden
verb	shows action	gave
direct object	receives action of verb	wave, wink
indirect object	receives object of giving and telling verbs	me
prepositional phrase	a group of words beginning with a preposition and ending with a noun or pronoun	in the garden

Case

Nouns and pronouns have different **jobs** to do in a sentence. Here is an example.

John is my friend. He is loyal. I like him. His dog is lost.

He is a subject, *him* is an object, and *his* shows possession. *He, him,* and *his* are different **forms** of the same word. Each **form** has a different **job**.

Form	Job
he	subject
him	object
his	possession

We would not say "Him is loyal" and "I like he." We know without thinking how to use each **form** for the right **job**. **Case** is another word for **job**. Here is the chart above with the case names.

Case	Form	Job
Nominative	he	subject
Objective	him	object
Possessive	his	shows possession

If a word is in the **nominative case**, it has the **job** of being a **subject**. If a word is in the **objective case**, it has the **job** of being an **object**. In Latin there are five cases. Here are the cases and the jobs of each.

Case Name	Job	English
Nominative	subject	
Genitive	possession	's, of
Dative	indirect object	to, for
Accusative	direct object	
Ablative	separation, location, means	in/by/with/from

Notice that the possessive case in English is called the genitive case in Latin; and the objective case in English is called the accusative case in Latin.

Number

In Latin and English grammar, there are two numbers: **singular** and **plural**. **Singular** means *one*; **plural** means *more than one*.

John and Mary are my friends. They are loyal. I like them. Their dog is lost.

They, them, and *their* are the plural forms of *he, him* and *his*. In English we usually add an **s** to make a noun plural: *girl* and *girls*. But some words, such as *man* and *men, child* and *children*, and *he* and *they*, have special forms for the plural.

Declension

Here is a Latin noun listed with all of its case forms in the singular and plural, with an example of the job that each noun is performing. The noun is **rosa**, *rose*.

Case and Number	Form	Possible Meaning	Job
nominative singular	rosa	The rose is red	subject
genitive singular	rosae	scent of the rose, the rose's scent	possession
dative singular	rosae	water for the rose	indirect object
accusative singular	rosam	I picked a rose	direct object
ablative singular	rosā	I got stuck by the rose	means (how)
nominative plural	rosae	The roses grew tall	subject
genitive plural	rosarum	color of roses	quality
dative plural	rosis	talking to the roses	indirect object
accusative plural	rosas	I smell the roses	direct object
ablative plural	rosis	We saw a bee in the roses	location

You will notice that some of the case forms are the same, and that most cases have more than one job. The context of the sentence helps to clarify the precise job of each word.

A **declension** is a table of all the **case forms** of a word, singular and plural. Here is the declension table of the English pronoun *he*.

Case	Singular	Plural	Function
Nominative	he	they	subject
Objective	him	them	object
Possessive	his	their	possession

Writing a noun with all of its forms in a chart is called **declining** a noun. **Incline** goes up and **decline** goes down. The word "decline" comes from the idea of stepping down from the most basic form of a word to the other forms.

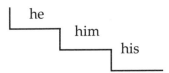

Below is a declension table for the Latin noun **mensa**. It steps down from the dictionary form, **mensa**, through all of the other forms **mensa** can be written in.

First Declension

Case	Singular	Ending	Plural	Ending
Nominative	*mens* **a**	-a	*mens* **ae**	-ae
Genitive	*mens* **ae**	-ae	*mens* **arum**	-arum
Dative	*mens* **ae**	-ae	*mens* **is**	-is
Accusative	*mens* **am**	-am	*mens* **as**	-as
Ablative	*mens* **ā**	-ā	*mens* **is**	-is

In Latin there are five families or declensions of nouns. **Mensa** is in the First Declension, and all of the nouns in that declension are declined like **mensa**. All the nouns in a family of nouns have the same or similar endings when they are declined.

Gender

Nouns can be identified as having gender. The words *he, him, his, king, uncle, son,* and *John* are said to be **masculine** because they refer to male persons. The words *she, her, queen, mother, sister,* and *Mary* are said to be **feminine** because they refer to female persons. Words that refer to non-living things, like *rock, table, sun,* and *hope,* have no gender and are said to be **neuter**.

Latin has the **natural** gender, described above, but it also has **grammatical** gender. In **grammatical** gender, non-living things which have no gender are labeled masculine or feminine. Most European languages are like Latin and have grammatical gender: French, German, Spanish, Italian, Russian.

Here are some Spanish words that have grammatical gender:

La Paz   El Paso

La means *the* for a feminine noun. **El** means *the* for a masculine noun. *La Paz* is the capital of Bolivia. *Paz* means peace. *Paz* is feminine even though peace is a thing. It has grammatical gender. *El Paso* is a city in Texas. *Paso* means passage or gateway. *Paso* is a *thing,* but it is masculine in Spanish. *Paz* and *Paso* have grammatical gender.

In Latin, **rosa** is feminine. A rose is a thing, but in Latin it is feminine; it has grammatical gender.

The abbreviations for gender are:

feminine	*f.*
masculine	*m.*
neuter	*n.*

Here are some other nouns in Latin that have grammatical gender. They are all non-living things, but they are identified as masculine or feminine.

mensa	*f.*	*table*		**lux**	*f.*	*light*
mundus	*m.*	*world*		**lacus**	*m.*	*lake*

♦ English and Latin don't have a one-to-one correspondence between their verb tenses. Beginning students should memorize a meaning for each Latin tense. Later they will study them more thoroughly to learn how to translate correctly between the two languages. English often has a verb phrase of 2-4 words that requires only one word in Latin.

♦ English has progressive forms in every tense to show continuous action; Latin does not.

♦ The main difficulty lies in the English past and the Latin perfect and imperfect. Study carefully the second and fourth rows, the English past and present perfect. Notice that the simple past in English, *I called every hour*, requires the imperfect tense in Latin.

English Tenses	Examples	Use in Latin and English	Corresponding Latin Tenses and Examples
Present System			

Present
  Simple
  Progressive
  Emphatic
	I *call* home.
	I *am calling* now.
	I *do call*.
		• General statement
		• Ongoing present action
		• Emphasis
			Present
			      Voco

Past
  Simple
 	
  Progressive
  Emphatic
	I *called* home.
	I *called* every hour.
	
	I *was calling*.
	I *did call*.
		• Indefinite past time
		• Repeated past action
		• Ongoing past action
		• Emphasis
			Perfect **Vocavi**
			Imperfect **Vocabam**
			Imperfect **Vocabam**
			Perfect **Vocavi**

Future Progressive	I *will call*. I *will be calling*.	• Future action	Future **Vocabo**
Perfect System			
Present Perfect Progressive	I *have called*. I *have been calling* all day.	• Completed action with respect to a present action, or a past action continuing to the present	Perfect **Vocavi** (N.B. The Latin perfect tenses do not have a progressive sense.)

Past Perfect
  Progressive
	I *had called* when you arrived.
	I *had been calling*.
		• Completed action with respect to a past action	Pluperfect
			      Vocaveram

Future Perfect
  Progressive
	I *will have called*.
	I *will have been calling*.
		• A future action completed with respect to another future action	Future Perfect
			      Vocavero

The term "classical pronunciation" refers to modern scholarship's best guess at how Latin may have been pronounced by the educated elite in the late Republic. This guide may be used instead of the Christian pronunciation guide provided in the front of the book.

Vowels

Vowels are either long or short. To keep from cluttering the text, we did not mark each vowel. In practice, it is best to listen to the classical pronunciation audio available from Memoria Press (www.memoriapress.com) to learn the correct vowel sound.

long	as in	example	short	as in	example
ā	father	fráter	a*	again	mensa
ē	late	sêdês	e	let	et
ī	seen	amîcus	i	sit	cibus
ō	open	nômen	o	offer	novem
ū	food	lûna	u	foot	sum

* When short **a** is in a stressed (accented) syllable, it is pronounced like long **ā**.

Diphthongs are long.

Diphthong	as in	example
ae	bite	caelum
oe	boil	proelium
au	cow	laudo

Consonants

Consonants are pronounced as in English, with the following exceptions:

bs	always pronounced *ps*	urbs
c	always hard: *cat*	voco, cibus
g	always hard: *go*	fuga, tergi
sc	always hard: *escape*	scribo, discipulus
h	always pronounced *h* except in transliteration of Greek letters (**th, ch, ph**)	hora, mihi /t-h/: theatrum, /k-h/: chorus, /p-h/: phalanx
qu	as in *quit*	equus, qui
s	as *sing* (never as *z*)	mensa, misi
t	as in *test*	nuntius
v	as *w* in *west*	verbum (**v** is sometimes written as **u**)

ORAL DRILLS

FOR LESSONS
III, V, IX, X, XIV, XVIII, & XXII

LESSON III

Oral Drill

1. salutas *you greet*	1. they will sail
2. superabit	2. I was freeing
3. ambulabunt	3. she will judge
4. líberat	4. we will walk
5. judicabo	5. they look at
6. adorabam	6. I was working
7. navigábitis	7. you will overcome
8. habitabat	8. he will adore
9. occupábimus	9. we are dwelling
10. laborabant	10. he greets

LESSON V

Oral Drill

1. ero	1. they were
2. eratis	2. you will be
3. erunt	3. we are
4. erat	4. she was
5. sumus	5. it will be
6. érimus	6. we were
7. es	7. you (p) will be
8. éritis	8. it is
9. eramus	9. I will be
10. eram	10. we will be

LESSON IX

Oral Drill

1.	**dubitáveras**	1.	I had hidden
2.	**negaveramus**	2.	she had thought
3.	**voláverat**	3.	we had doubted
4.	**putáveram**	4.	they had denied
5.	**speráverant**	5.	he had asked
6.	**mutáverat**	6.	you (p) had disturbed
7.	**celaveratis**	7.	you had changed
8.	**perturbáveram**	8.	it had flown
9.	**accusáveras**	9.	they had accused
10.	**rogáverant**	10.	I had hoped

LESSON X

Oral Drill

1.	**nuntiáverint**	1.	I will have wounded
2.	**explorávero**	2.	you will have explored
3.	**demonstravéritis**	3.	we will have delighted
4.	**oppugnáveris**	4.	she will have pointed out
5.	**creavéritis**	5.	they will have created
6.	**culpavérimus**	6.	you (p) will have expected
7.	**exspectáverint**	7.	he will have attacked
8.	**appellávero**	8.	we will have blamed
9.	**vulneravérimus**	9.	I will have addressed
10.	**delectáveris**	10.	they will have reported

LESSON XIV

Oral Drill - Nominative Case

1.	agrícolae	1.	girl
2.	nauta	2.	poet
3.	terra	3.	farmer
4.	puellae	4.	sailors
5.	mensa	5.	lands
6.	Itália	6.	tables
7.	reginae	7.	Mary
8.	Maria	8.	Rome
9.	Roma	9.	Italy
10.	poetae	10.	queen

LESSON XVIII

Oral Drill - Nominative Case

1.	annus bonus	1.	high heaven
2.	nautae novi	2.	wide kingdom
3.	poeta malus	3.	bad master
4.	parvae mensae	4.	large worlds
5.	multa dona	5.	small sins
6.	magnus equus	6.	much land
7.	amici aeterni	7.	many lands
8.	latum forum	8.	new farmer
9.	alta templa	9.	holy words
10.	regina sancta	10.	good sons

LESSON XXII

Oral Drill - Nominative Case

1. **luces**	1. soldier
2. **panis**	2. soldiers
3. **sol**	3. feet
4. **cruces**	4. sister
5. **mílites**	5. cross
6. **miles**	6. laws
7. **pedes**	7. voices
8. **vox**	8. dogs
9. **dux**	9. sun
10. **pes**	10. customs

VOCABULARY

accuso (1)	to accuse	equus -i m.*	horse
adoro (1)*	to adore	erro (1)	to err, wander
adventus -ūs m.	arrival	exércitus -ūs m.	army
aeternus -a -um*	eternal, everlasting	exploro (1)	to explore
agnus -i m.*	lamb	exspecto (1)	to wait for, expect
agrícola -ae m.	farmer	fácies -ei f.	face
altus -a -um*	high, deep	fides -ei f.	faith, trust
ámbulo (1)*	to walk	fílius -i m.*	son
amicus -i m.*	friend	flumen flúminis n.*	river
amo (1)*	to love, like	forum -i n.*	forum, marketplace
annus -i m.*	year	frater fratris m.*	brother
appáreo (2)	to appear	fructus -ūs m.	fruit
appello (1)*	to address	gáudeo -ēre -- --	to rejoice
árdeo -ēre arsi arsus	to burn, be on fire	hábeo (2)*	to have
aro (1)	to plow	hábito (1)*	to live in, dwell
bellum -i n.*	war	heri	yesterday
bonus -a -um*	good	hódie	today
caelum -i n.*	sky, heaven	Itália -ae f.*	Italy
canis canis m. or f.*	dog	júbeo -ēre jussi jussus*	to order, command
caput cápitis n.*	head	júdico (1)*	to judge, consider
cáveo -ēre cavi cautus	to beware of, guard against	juvo juvare juvi jutus	to help
		laboro (1)*	to work
celo (1)*	to hide	lacus -ūs m.	lake
Christus -i m.*	Christ	latus -a -um	wide, broad
clamo (1)*	to shout	laudo (1)*	to praise
cor cordis n.	heart	lavo lavare lavi lautus*	to wash
cras	tomorrow	lex legis f.*	law
creo (1)	to create	líbero (1)*	to set free
crux crucis f.*	cross	lumen lúminis n.	lamp
culpo (1)	to blame	lux lucis f.*	light
débeo (2)*	to owe, ought	magnus -a -um*	great, large
débitum -i n.*	debt, sin	malus -a -um*	bad
decem*	ten	máneo -ēre mansi mansus	to remain, stay
décimus -a -um	tenth	manus -ūs f.	hand
delecto (1)	to delight, please	Maria -ae f.*	Mary
demonstro (1)	to show, point out	mater matris f.*	mother
deus -i m.*	god	mensa -ae f.*	table
dies -ei m.	day	metus -ūs m.	fear
do dare dedi datus*	to give	miles mílitis m.*	soldier
dóceo -ēre dócui doctus*	to teach	móneo (2)*	to warn
dóminus -i m.*	lord, master	mos moris m.	custom
domus -ūs f.	house, home	móveo -ēre movi motus*	to move
donum -i n.*	gift	multus -a -um*	much, many
dúbito (1)	to doubt	mundus -i m.*	world, mankind
duo*	two	muto (1)	to change
dux ducis m.	leader	narro (1)*	to tell

nato (1)	to swim	Roma -ae f.*	Rome
nauta -ae m.*	sailor	saepe*	often
návigo (1)*	to sail	saluto (1)	to greet
nego (1)	to deny	sanctus -a -um*	sacred, holy
nomen nóminis n.*	name	saxum -i n.	rock
non*	not	secundus -a -um*	second
nonus -a -um	ninth	sédeo -ēre sedi sessus*	to sit
novem*	nine	semper*	always
novus -a -um*	new	senatus -ūs m.	senate
numquam*	never	septem*	seven
nunc*	now	séptimus -a -um	seventh
núntio (1)	to report	servo (1)	to guard, keep
óccupo (1)*	to seize	servus -i m.*	slave, servant
octavus -a -um	eighth	sex*	six
octo*	eight	sextus -a -um	sixth
óppidum -i n.*	town	sol solis m.	sun
oppugno (1)	to attack	soror sororis f.*	sister
opto (1)	to desire, wish	specto (1)*	to look at
oro (1)*	to speak, pray	spero (1)	to hope
panis panis m.	bread	spes -ei f.	hope
paro (1) *	to prepare	spíritus -ūs m.	spirit
parvus -a -um*	small	sto stare steti status	to stand
pater patris m.*	father	sum esse fui futurus	to be
pax pacis f.*	peace	súpero (1)*	to overcome, surpass
perturbo (1)	to disturb	táceo (2)	to be silent
pes pedis m.	foot	templum -i n.	temple
poeta -ae m.	poet	tempto (1)	to tempt
porto (1)*	to carry	téneo -ēre ténui tentus	to hold
portus -ūs m.	harbor	terra -ae f.*	earth, land
primus -a -um*	first	térreo (2)*	to frighten
prohíbeo (2)	to prevent	tértius -a -um*	third
puella -ae f.*	girl	tímeo -ēre tímui --*	to fear, be afraid of
pugno (1)*	to fight	tres*	three
puto (1)	to think	tum	then, at that time
quartus -a -um	fourth	umquam	ever
quattuor*	four	unus -a -um*	one
quinque*	five	váleo -ēre válui --	to be strong, be well
quintus -a -um	fifth	*verbum -i n.*	word
regina -ae f.*	queen	vídeo -ēre vidi visus*	to see
regnum -i n.*	kingdom	voco (1)*	to call
res -ei f.	thing, matter, affair, business	volo (1)	to fly
		vox vocis f.*	voice
respondeo -ēre		vúlnero (1)	to wound
respondi responsus	to respond, answer		
rex regis m.*	king		
rogo (1)	to ask		

*Vocabulary included in *Latina Christiana*, 4th Edition*

accuse	accuso (1)	earth	terra -ae f.
address	appello (1)	eight	octo
adore	adoro (1)	eighth	octavus -a -um
affair	res -ei f.	err	erro (1)
always	semper	eternal	aeternus -a -um
answer	respondeo ēre respondi responsus	ever	umquam
		everlasting	aeternus -a -um
appear	appáreo (2)	expect	exspecto (1)
army	exércitus -ūs m.	explore	exploro (1)
arrival	adventus -ūs m.	face	fácies -ei f.
ask	rogo (1)	faith	fides -ei f.
attack	oppugno (1)	farmer	agrícola -ae m.
at that time	tum	father	pater patris m.
bad	malus -a -um	fear (noun)	metus -ūs m.
be	sum esse fui futurus	fear (verb)	tímeo -ēre timui --
be afraid of	tímeo -ēre tímui --	fifth	quintus -a -um
be on fire	árdeo -ēre arsi arsus	fight	pugno (1)
be silent	táceo (2)	first	primus -a -um
be strong	váleo -ēre válui --	five	quinque
be well	váleo -ēre válui --	fly	volo (1)
beware of	cáveo -ēre cavi cautus	foot	pes pedis m.
blame	culpo (1)	forum	forum -i n.
bread	panis panis m.	four	quattuor
broad	latus -a -um	fourth	quartus -a -um
brother	frater fratris m.	friend	amicus -i m.
burn	árdeo -ēre arsi arsus	frighten	térreo (2)
business	res -ei f.	fruit	fructus -ūs m.
call	voco (1)	gift	donum -i n.
carry	porto (1)	girl	puella -ae f.
change	muto (1)	give	do dare dedi datus
Christ	Christus -i m.	god	deus -i m.
command	júbeo -ēre jussi jussus	good	bonus -a -um
consider	júdico (1)	great	magnus -a -um
create	creo (1)	greet	saluto (1)
cross	crux crucis f.	guard	servo (1)
custom	mos moris m.	guard against	cáveo -ēre cavi cautus
day	dies -ei m.	hand	manus -ūs f.
debt	débitum -i n.	harbor	portus -ūs m.
deep	altus -a -um	have	hábeo (2)
delight	delecto (1)	head	caput cápitis n.
deny	nego (1)	heart	cor cordis n.
desire	opto (1)	heaven	caelum -i n.
disturb	perturbo (1)	help	juvo juvare juvi jutus
dog	canis canis m. or f.	hide	celo (1)
doubt	dúbito (1)	high	altus -a -um
dwell	hábito (1)	hold	téneo -ēre ténui tentus

holy	sanctus -a -um
home	domus -ūs f.
hope (noun)	spes -ei f.
hope (verb)	spero (1)
horse	equus -i m.
house	domus -ūs f.
Italy	Itália -ae f.
judge	júdico (1)
keep	servo (1)
king	rex regis m.
kingdom	regnum -i n.
lake	lacus -ūs m.
lamb	agnus -i m.
lamp	lumen lúminis n.
land	terra -ae f.
large	magnus -a -um
law	lex legis f.
leader	dux ducis m.
light	lux lucis f.
like	amo (1)
live in	hábito (1)
look at	specto (1)
lord	dóminus -i m.
love	amo (1)
mankind	mundus -i m.
many	multi -ae -a (plural)
marketplace	forum -i n.
Mary	Maria -ae f.
master	dóminus -i m.
matter	res -ei f.
mother	mater matris f.
move	móveo -ēre movi motus
much	multus -a -um (sing)
name	nomen nóminis n.
never	numquam
new	novus -a -um
nine	novem
ninth	nonus -a -um
not	non
now	nunc
often	saepe
one	unus -a -um
order	júbeo -ēre jussi jussus
ought	débeo (2)
overcome	súpero (1)
owe	débeo (2)

peace	pax pacis f.
please	delecto (1)
plow	aro (1)
poet	poeta -ae m.
point out	demonstro (1)
praise	laudo (1)
pray	oro (1)
prepare	paro (1)
prevent	prohíbeo (2)
queen	regina -ae f.
rejoice	gáudeo -ēre -- --
remain	máneo -ēre mansi mansus
report	núntio (1)
respond	respóndeo -ēre respondi responsus
river	flumen flúminis n.
rock	saxum -i n.
Rome	Roma -ae f.
sacred	sanctus -a -um
sail	návigo (1)
sailor	nauta -ae m.
second	secundus -a -um
see	vídeo -ēre vidi visus
seize	óccupo (1)
senate	senatus -ūs m.
servant	servus -i m.
set free	líbero (1)
seven	septem
seventh	séptimus -a -um
shout	clamo (1)
show	demonstro (1)
sin	débitum -i n.
sister	soror sororis f.
sit	sédeo -ēre sedi sessus
six	sex
sixth	sextus -a -um
sky	caelum -i n.
slave	servus -i m.
small	parvus -a -um
soldier	miles mílitis m.
son	fílius -i m.
speak	oro (1)
spirit	spíritus -ūs m.
stand	sto stare steti status
stay	máneo -ēre mansi mansus
sun	sol solis m.

surpass	súpero (1)
swim	nato (1)
table	mensa -ae f.
teach	dóceo -ēre dócui doctus
tell	narro (1)
temple	templum -i n.
tempt	tempto (1)
ten	decem
tenth	décimus -a -um
then	tum
thing	res -ei f.
think	puto (1)
third	tértius -a -um
three	tres
today	hódie
tomorrow	cras
town	óppidum -i n.
trust	fides -ei f.
two	duo
voice	vox vocis f.
wait for	exspecto (1)
walk	ámbulo (1)
wander	erro (1)
war	bellum -i n.
warn	móneo (2)
wash	lavo lavare lavi lautus
wide	latus -a -um
wish	opto (1)
word	verbum -i n.
work	laboro (1)
world	mundus -i m.
wound	vúlnero (1)
year	annus -i m.
yesterday	heri

[1] In this course, long vowels are marked only to distinguish certain grammatical forms, such as the ablative singular ending in the first declension (**mensā**), the infinitive of the second conjugation (**monēre**), and the genitive singular, nominative and accusative plural of the fourth declension (**portūs**).

[2] The present stem is derived from the infinitive; Lesson IV has a fuller treatment of the present stem.

[3] The 4th principal part can be written with the ending **um** or **us**. This text uses **us** because that is consistent with the dictionary form for adjectives and the 4th principal part is a participle (verbal adjective). The Henle text uses **us** for transitive verbs and **um** for intransitive verbs, but this text is not making that distinction at this point.

[4] The general rule for finding the stem of Latin nouns is to "drop the ending of the genitive singular." This rule will be given in lesson XXI when students can see the reason for it.

[5] The nominative singular ending is a short vowel and the ablative singular ending is long. The use of the macron here is to help students recognize the different cases in writing, not to make a pronunciation distinction between long and short vowels, which we are not emphasizing in this text.

[6] **Caelum** is masculine in the plural: **caeli -orum**.

[7] Forms of **unus** and **tres** will be used in cases where they are regular.

[8] The 3rd declension also has **i-stem** nouns which will be covered in *Second Form*.